TONY STEWART

FROM INDY PHENOM TO NASCAR SUPERSTAR

JOHN CLOSE
AND THE EDITORS OF
STOCK CAR RACING MAGAZINE

MOTORBOOKS
INTERNATIONAL

This edition first published in 2004 by Motorbooks International, an imprint of MBI Publishing Company, Galtier Plaza, Suite 200, 380 Jackson Street, St. Paul, MN 55101-3885 USA

The information in this book is true and complete to the best of our knowledge. All recommendations are made without any guarantee on the part of the author or Publisher, who also disclaim any liability incurred in connection with the use of this data or specific details.

Motorbooks International titles are also available at discounts in bulk quantity for industrial or sales-promotional use. For details write to Special Sales Manager at Motorbooks International Wholesalers & Distributors, Galtier Plaza, Suite 200, 380 Jackson Street, St. Paul, MN 55101-3885 USA.

ISBN 0-7603-1855-7

On the front cover: Tony Stewart takes a moment before each race to think about the task ahead. *Nigel Kinrade*

On the frontis: Despite his earned reputation for being hostile to the media, Stewart does sometimes offer photographers a smile behind the wheel. *Harold Hinson*

On the title page: Stewart leading the pack at Bristol. *Nigel Kinrade*

On the back cover: Stewart still dreams about winning an Indy 500 race, but has focused more on his stock car racing career in the last few years. **Main photo:** *Harold Hinson* **Inset photo:** *Frank Mormillo*

About the author: John Close has been writing about NASCAR since 1986, when he covered his first Winston Cup race at Bristol, Tennessee. Since then, Close, a Wisconsin native, has staffed countless NASCAR events as a journalist, public relations and marketing specialist, team manager, and race day spotter.

His work has appeared in numerous racing publications, including *Stock Car Racing* and *Circle Track* magazines, *Winston Cup Scene*, and *Winston Cup Illustrated*.

He and his wife, Gail, live in Charlotte, North Carolina. They have a son, Sam, who is in college.

Editor: Leah Noel
Contributing Editor: Glen Grissom
Designed by Katie Sonmor

Printed in China

Contents

Introduction
Tony Stewart: Another A. J. 7

Section 1 **The Open-Wheel Years** 10

Tony Stewart:
The Hottest Open-Wheel Driver in America
By Dave Argabright, *Open Wheel*, March 1996 13

The Mickyard 200:
The IRL Opens Up with Rookies Looking Like Real Race Car Drivers
Staff Report, *Open Wheel*, May 1996 30

The Graduates
Staff Report, *Open Wheel*, February 1998 40

Section 2 **The Jump to Stock Cars** 52

Stewart Comes to NASCAR
By Bruce Martin, *Circle Track*, February 1997 54

The Recruitment of Tony Stewart
By Bruce Martin, *Stock Car Racing*, July 1999 62

Tony Stewart: Just Another Rookie or
the Greatest Thing Since Sliced Bread?
By Bob Myers, *Stock Car Racing*, July 1999 73

A Rookie Report: A Look Back at Daytona
By Tony Stewart, *Circle Track*, July 1999 81

Recapping Stewart's First Cup Season:
1999 Raybestos ROY Rises in Winston Cup
Staff Report, *Circle Track*, February 2000 85

Section 3   **Roots** 92

    Playing in the Sand:
    Tony Stewart Toyed with Everyone at the Copper World Classic
    Staff Report, *Open Wheel*, May 1998 .95

    The Pain of Pure Desire
    Staff Report, *Open Wheel*, September 1998 101

Section 4   **The Drive to Win Fuels a Temper** 106

    Tony's World
    By Ron Lemasters Jr., *Open Wheel*, June 2000 109

    Temper, Temper:
    If You Want to Come to the Party, Be Prepared to Dance
    By Bob Myers, *Circle Track*, November 2000 113

    Tony Tirades
    By Benny Phillips, *Stock Car Racing*, March 2003 120

Section 5   **Success in Winston Cup** 124

    The *Stock Car* Interview:
    Tony Stewart
    By Jason Mitchell, *Stock Car Racing*, November 2002 127

    Winning Is the Best Medicine
    By Bob Myers, *Circle Track*, April 2003 138

    One at a Time:
    Stewart's Failure to Repeat as Champ Is a NASCAR Trend
    By Larry Cothren, *Stock Car Racing*, November 2003 144

    Epilogue
    Gazing into the Future 156

    Stewart's Career Statistics 158

    Index 159

Introduction

Tony Stewart: Another A. J.

With championships in USAC, IRL, and NASCAR, Tony Stewart has proven to be both versatile and a winner. *Nigel Kinrade*

Anthony Joseph Foyt—"A. J." to the racing world—is arguably the greatest driver to ever strap on a race car, any race car.

Foyt was the master of all things on four wheels. The legendary Texan won the Indianapolis 500 four times, both in a front- and rear-engine car. On his way through the ranks to Indy car fame, no midget, sprint, or champ car could throw "Super Tex" as he recorded 52 career United States Auto Club (USAC) victories in those divisions. The 1972 Daytona 500, the Super Bowl of stock car racing, is counted among his seven career NASCAR wins, as are 41 career USAC stock car victories. Even the 1967 LeMans Sports car classic proved no match for the driver, whose temper at times proved to be as epic as his driving skills.

Today, no driver embodies the talent and temperament of Foyt more than Tony Stewart. In fact, Foyt was among the first to recognize Stewart's ability behind the wheel and desire to succeed away from it. He almost hired the young charger to drive his Indy car entry after an off-season test at Phoenix in 1995.

Had it not been for the passing of a couple of generations, Tony Stewart and Foyt might have been furious on-track rivals. Like Foyt, Stewart has proven to be a master in just about every type of racer he buckles himself into. USAC midget, sprint, and champ car titles, an Indy Racing League (IRL) crown, and a NASCAR Winston Cup championship are among Stewart's accomplishments. His racing resume is already Hall of Fame caliber, and he is just in his early 30s.

One can only imagine the on-track tire-smoking, fender-rubbing thrills Stewart and Foyt may have provided, not to mention the off-track tirades the pair would have enacted. To say that victory is the only thing that matters to each of these drivers is almost an understatement.

The comparison of Stewart to Foyt is an easy one. Relaxed with their inner circle friends, contentious with the media, driven beyond expectation on the racetrack, the drivers mirror each other despite their ages and the leap of time between them. Even Foyt could see the comparison.

Considered by many to be the greatest driver in motorsports history, A. J. Foyt captured the imagination of the fans with his desire to win on the track and his temperament off the track. Many today see those same qualities in Tony Stewart. *John Close*

Like A. J. Foyt, Stewart's Holy Grail is the Indy 500. While Foyt won the race four times, Stewart has yet to see victory lane at the famed Brickyard. Here, he paces the field after winning the pole position for the 1996 classic. *Ken Coles*

"Tony Stewart is going back to the old style of race car drivers," Foyt stated in a 1997 interview for *Circle Track* magazine. "He wants to race. He wants to show the world how good he is. Tony will have to pick what series he wants to be in, but let's face it, he is going to be big wherever he goes."

There's no need for a "throwback" or "heritage" uniform here. Stewart, like Foyt, is a once-in-a-generation racer. That's why he's been a fan favorite and the subject of several stories in *Stock Car Racing*, *Circle Track*, and *Open Wheel* magazines over the years, many of which are included here for your reading pleasure.

We invite you to enjoy the ride from Stewart's early days in the midget ranks to his current status as one of the top drivers in all of motorsports. We guarantee it'll be a wild ride, both on and off the track.

— *John Close*

Stewart, like Foyt, isn't afraid to drive anything as evidenced by this photo, which shows him with a dirt late-model car prior to a 1997 Hav-A-Tampa event at Brownstown, Indiana.

A. J. Foyt won in all types of race cars, including stock cars. Here, Foyt is shown celebrating one of his seven NASCAR Cup Series wins with the famed Wood Brothers. *Bob Mangram*

The Open-Wheel Years

The eyes and the smile are the same, albeit a few more teeth are missing. Still, it's easy to recognize the 10-year-old go kart driver is Tony Stewart. There's a familiarity in the face, but more important, there's a comfort, an easiness the youngster exudes as he sits in his kart surrounded by trophies he's won. It's like he belongs there.

From the start, Stewart felt right at home behind the wheel of a high-powered go kart. He began his racing career at age seven and, with the help of his father, quickly began winning races on oval tracks around his native Rushville, Indiana. He also quickly learned that he doesn't like to finish second.

By 1983, Stewart was the driver to beat at each event and won his first racing title of any kind—the International Karting Federation (IKF) Grand National

Stewart got his start in racing in the go kart ranks and made his first big splash in the USAC midget ranks. Here, Stewart looks pensive before a 1993 midget event. *Bill Zimbiski*

championship. Over the next three years Stewart matured as a driver, spending his teen years winning countless go kart events throughout the Midwest. By age 16, Stewart added another crown, a World Karting Association (WKA) national championship, to his list of accomplishments. It was only the beginning of what was to become a legendary career in open-wheel racing.

Above
Stewart (4) started on the pole for the 1993 Hut Hundred at Terre Haute, Indiana, and out-battled Stan Fox for the win in the prestigious event. Here, Stewart takes the green flag alongside Page Jones (1) and Brian Gerster (21) in a rousing start. *John Mahoney*

Right
It didn't take long for Stewart to become a regular winner in the midget ranks. This is a victory lane shot after Stewart captured a midget event at Terre Haute, Indiana, in June 1993. Pictured here are (from left) third-place driver Steve Knepper, Melissa McCammon, Stewart, Melanie McCammon, and runner-up Page Jones. *Jim Cooling*

Roy Barker was one of the first to recognize Stewart's talent. The veteran car owner was impressed with Stewart's go kart prowess and gave the 18-year-old driver a shot at piloting a three-quarter (TQ) midget. In just his third start in the car, Stewart didn't disappoint and captured the checkered flag in a race.

Stewart built on his midget success in the early 1990s, winning the 1991 USAC Rookie of the Year midget title and scoring his first midget win at the famed Indianapolis Speedrome in 1991. That same year, Stewart jumped to the larger, more powerful USAC sprint car ranks. He won his first race in that division in 1992 at I-44 Speedway in Missouri.

Back in the midgets, Stewart made his first-ever start on a dirt surface a memorable one when he flipped his mount on lap nine of the 1992 Hut Hundred at Terre Haute, Indiana. Undaunted, Stewart showed the dogged racing resolve that later became his career trademark by rejoining the event and finishing sixth. A year later, Stewart won the Hut Hundred classic, his first-ever USAC national midget victory.

The 1994 season brought more success to Stewart. He captured his first USAC national midget title by winning five times in 22 starts. For his efforts, Stewart was one of just 12 drivers to be named to the American Auto Racing Writers and Broadcasters 25th Anniversary All-American Team.

In the next five years, Stewart's career continued its meteoric rise. He shined in the USAC midget, sprint, and champ car ranks. He became one of the brightest stars of a new racing body—the Indy Racing League—and took on the greatest race of them all, the Indianapolis 500. Stock car racing and NASCAR weren't even in the picture yet.

Stewart won the 1994 USAC midget championship and earned the right to sport the No. 1 on his car in 1995. Stewart is shown here battling the 1994 points runner-up, Andy Michner, in a 1995 USAC midget event at Winchester, Indiana. *Jim Cooling*

Tony Stewart

The Hottest Open-Wheel Driver in America

By Dave Argabright
Open Wheel, March 1996

It is good to dream, to allow the imagination to wander frivolously and present those far-fetched, wild ideas that you know deep down will never come to pass.

In early 1995, Tony Stewart dreamed big. He was the defending USAC midget champion, but he wanted more. Wouldn't it be awesome, he thought, to win the USAC Silver Crown, sprint, and midget titles? How about winning them all in the same year?

It was a dream that came true.

Running for all three titles simultaneously has been talked about for years. After all, many USAC drivers have excelled in all three divisions. But the logistics in the past were so nightmarish that seeing a driver race for, let alone win, two titles in a single year was rare.

But when USAC announced its schedules early in 1995, it was obvious that the possibilities for multiple championships had increased. Very few direct conflicts between races existed, so it became technically possible to get it done.

Still, winning a USAC title in any year and in any division is extremely difficult. Racing against seasoned drivers and mechanics, with specs more tightly controlled than any short-track open-wheel division in the country, on both dirt and asphalt, brings about extremely tight point races that are generally the rule and not the exception.

Be careful what you dream of, your dreams just might come true.
— Unknown

So, while the schedule was certainly more favorable for a broad-fronted assault than in the past, any USAC veteran would point out that going into the season nobody could expect a championship in any division, even if the whole package of driver, equipment, funding, and team were all together.

When Stewart began plotting his season, he realized that he had a good opportunity, given the quality of equipment he had under him in all three divisions. He began the year at Phoenix, racing the Potter midget and the Niebel/Boles Silver Crown car. He and Niebel, who had also hired Stewart for his sprint car, had discussed the chances of chasing points in all three divisions, and Niebel was a bit of a skeptic.

"I was very much concerned about the potential conflicts," admitted Niebel, who marked his 30th season as a car owner last year. "I wanted somebody focused on our deal, but I knew what Tony was trying to accomplish. What we finally agreed to was that Tony would look at the points situation later in the year and decide at that time what he needed to do if there were conflicts. And that seemed fair enough."

With the limited number of direct conflicts, Stewart figured the travel requirements for all three divisions would be manageable. After all, in 1994 he had attempted to win the USAC national midget title, as well as the Western States division (he eventually won the national title, but not the Western States crown). That, girlfriend/advisor/travel agent Amanda Keaton said, was a real challenge.

"Trying to arrange travel in 1994 was a real nightmare. It wasn't just the distance, but the time difference. Plus, there were lots of conflicts and lots of red-eye flights. Since there were so few

By 1995, Tony Stewart was the master of the "slide job" as evidenced by this action at the Chili Bowl in Tulsa, Oklahoma. *Dave Olson*

Stewart (1) battles the legendary Stan Fox (15) in the same race. *Boyd Adams*

scheduled conflicts this year, we really felt like we could manage the travel part of it," Keaton said.

"It turned out this year that the travel part of it was not a problem at all."

So Tony Stewart began the 1995 season determined to give the triple crown a real shot. Although just 24, he knew very well what he was doing. After all, he had 16 years of racing experience behind him. He'd begun his career in go karts at age eight, running Muncie and Crawfordsville, Indiana, and his hometown of Columbus, where he eventually won eight track championships before age 19. He scored an amazing upset to win the 1983 IKF Dirt Grand Nationals at Oskaloosa, Iowa, his first national title. In 1986 he won the WKA national point championship on a road course.

All those wins came aboard his dad Nelson's kart. But by 1987, they were burned out, broke, and frustrated.

"We were out of money, buying junk tires, stuff like that, and we both had just had it," recalled Tony. "I told Dad that if we can't do it right, let's just quit."

"It was a difficult time," Nelson admitted.

They took the rest of the season off, deciding to focus on a good start in 1988. They had a good year and decided that the next logical step was a three-quarter (TQ) midget for 1989.

Stewart raced and won from coast to coast in capturing the 1995 USAC National Midget championship. Here, he poses (from left) with Billy Boat, a trophy queen, and Johnny Parsons after winning at Cal Expo Speedway near Sacramento in October of that year. *Dennis Mattish*

If Midwestern fans can boast that their area is the hub of sprint and midget racing, then surely Indiana is the world's capital of TQ racing. Drawing large crowds to small towns such as Greensburg, Warsaw, Madison, Columbus, and Rushville, the United Midget Racing Association (UMRA) series is an incredibly tough circuit where rookies just don't win.

But Stewart made his first start in the series in 1989 in Ray Barker's car and finished 20th. They missed the show the next time out. But on July 14, in his third TQ race, Stewart won in front of a grandstand packed with screaming race junkies at the mecca of TQ racing, Rushville. Before the year was out, he claimed 11 top-10 finishes in 17 starts, including 4 wins. It was clear that this kid was something special.

"I remember pitting next to them at Rushville," said Larry Martz, a hometown guy with a TQ of his own. "I was thinking, 'God, look at that scrawny little kid.' But that first night I saw him run, I knew there was something different about this kid. He was gonna be great. There just wasn't any doubt."

Martz and his family befriended Stewart, and he eventually spent seat time in Martz's TQ and later his midget. Stewart stayed at Martz's home in 1990, eventually adopting Rushville as his hometown.

In 1991, in addition to running the TQ circuit, Stewart began the transition to midgets and sprint cars. He made his debut in April aboard the Leary Boys midget at Winchester, where he finished 10th. In July, he finished seventh at Winchester in his first sprint feature, running Steve Chrisman's car.

In the next three years Stewart claimed 10 wins across the three national USAC divisions. In midgets, he eventually moved to the car of Rollie Helmling, with whom he won the Hut Hundred in 1993. In late 1993, he joined the Potter team and captured the national championship with the team

Stewart celebrated winning his three 1995 USAC National Championships by posing with the cars outside the Indianapolis Motor Speedway Museum. Stewart would later return to the facility in search of glory in the Indianapolis 500 and the Brickyard 400. *Steve Ellis, Indianapolis Motor Speedway*

in 1994. He earned USAC sprint Rookie of the Year honors in 1991 with Chrisman, later moving to the cars of both Ben Leyba and 6R racing.

For 1995, he felt confident. Niebel's sprint and Silver Crown cars featured potent V-6 engines and proven reliability. He and the Potter team were primed to repeat as midget champs.

But Stewart felt most confident in the sprint car, even though the V-6 is at a disadvantage on heavy dirt tracks.

"Of the three divisions, I thought we had our best shot at a championship in the sprint car, even with the V-6," Stewart said. "I knew how strong Glen's pavement program was. He was questioning a little bit about how we'd do on the dirt, but I've ran a lot on dirt, and I was confident we would do all right.

"The USAC sprints on dirt are even tougher than the pavement deal. When you go to places like Kokomo and race against guys like Brian Hayden and Kevin Thomas who run there every week, you'd better have your act together. But I felt like we would get it done."

Part of the uncertainty for both the sprint and Silver Crown effort centered on tires. Niebel is a longtime Hoosier loyalist, and they have supplied him with an excellent pavement tire. However, Hoosier's dirt program was far behind Goodyear and McCreary at the conclusion of the 1994 season. And when Niebel won the sprint feature (with Kevin Doty aboard) at the Eldora Four Crown Nationals in late 1994, he did so on McCrearys.

"I think people looked at us early [last] year, and looked at the fact that we were running a V-6 on Hoosier tires, and thought we were a joke," Niebel said. "But Hoosier really had their act together and developed a good tire, and it all started coming together. When the tires started working, we started winning races."

Indeed, Stewart and Niebel were immediately competitive and steadily improved. Early in the season there was a unique three-way tie among Stewart, Eric Gordon, and defending champ Doug Kalitta. Stewart began to pull ahead after wins at Indianapolis Raceway Park (IRP) in May and June, and at Santa Fe on July 28 he did the unthinkable: He beat the USAC's best on dirt with the little V-6 and Hoosiers.

"Everybody was shocked," Stewart said, "but I wasn't. I really believed we could win with that combination."

The pivotal race was at Tri-City Speedway in Granite City, Illinois, on September 3. Jack Hewitt was red hot on USAC dirt and was leading the feature when Stewart ran him down from deep in the pack to take the win.

"When you beat Jack Hewitt on dirt, you have absolutely done something," said Stewart. "When we caught him and beat him, that's when I thought we had it. I mean, he's my idol! He just doesn't miss."

Doug Kalitta, who had evolved to become Stewart's closest challenger, finished last at Granite City. The tide had turned.

After Granite City, Stewart won two of the final four USAC races, and his win at the Eldora Four Crown clinched the title. However, the car owner's title was still hotly contested between Niebel and 6R Racing (Hewitt). As Stewart was leading the feature, he saw the yellow light flip on and came upon the spun No. 63 of Hewitt.

"I felt bad for Jack, but I knew that would give Glen some breathing room on the owner's title," Stewart said. "I knew the driver's title was locked up, but I wanted so much to see that Glen got the owner's title as well."

In the finale at Winchester, in which the owner's title was clinched, Stewart was leading the feature when a right front wheel broke, slamming him hard into the outside wall. Still, it had been a great season, with seven sprint car wins.

Tony Stewart and Glen Niebel spent a lot of time together last summer, since they were running two divisions. At first, said Niebel, both had to make a big adjustment.

"Tony was younger and probably a little less mature than drivers I've had in my car in the past," Niebel said. "What that meant was that I had to adjust the way we did things a little bit, and I had to spend a lot more time talking with Tony and making sure we clearly understood one another.

"The biggest problem we had was he kept trying too hard and kept trying to overdrive the car. I kept talking to him and finally at the IRP Silver Crown race, I convinced him to relax and let the car work. And I think once he did that, it made him a better race driver in all the cars."

It was not an easy adjustment for Stewart. His anxiety rose early in the year until finally, two weeks before his 24th birthday in May, he left the Potter team. One week later, he was aboard Steve Lewis' Performance Racing Beast, with Bob East turning the wrenches.

"I know Tony grew up a lot this year, and I'd like to think that Bob [East] and I had a little bit to do with that," Niebel said. "I know I was very hard on him. I threatened to fire him several times, and that just didn't get his attention. Finally, I just told him, 'Hey, Tony, points or no points, if you don't think we're gettin' the job done, why don't you sit out for a week or so and let me put somebody else in the car?' Boy, that just set him on fire. He would get really focused then, and we would progress."

But while the Silver Crown effort stayed in the hunt, it was an incredibly close season. Dave Darland was the early division leader, with a surging Jack Hewitt capturing attention as the season moved into the stretch. Stewart failed to qualify for the Hoosier Hundred, which Darland won. Ironically, as the season wound down, the USAC Advisory Committee voted to ban the V-6 in Silver Crown racing for 1996, so it was obvious that it was now or never for the little powerplant.

At the Eldora Four Crown, Stewart dueled with Darland while Hewitt took a popular win. That left only Sacramento on the schedule.

The outlook for Stewart was not good as he made the trip west. He stood third in the standings, with Darland leading and Hewitt second. For Stewart to win the title, both would have to drop out while Stewart finished near the front. That was an unlikely scenario, given that Darland's machine was wrenched by Galen Fox and Hewitt had wizard Bob Hampshire in his pit.

"I went into that race thinking that if we finished in top three in points that was a pretty successful season," Stewart recalled. "It turned out to be like a storybook ending."

For Stewart, at least. For Darland and Hewitt, it was more like a horror story.

First to go away was Darland, who was leading when his engine expired, and he was singed by the spectacular oil fire that followed.

"I was right behind Hewitt when Dave went out," Stewart said. "We were in the top ten, and I got a good run off the corner and got past Jack in some traffic. I've got to give that night

Stewart's early success put him in the television spotlight, especially on ESPN, a network that featured weekly USAC midget and sprint car events. Here, ESPN broadcaster Dave Despain, Kenny Irwin, and Stewart watch a television replay after an event. *James Compton*

to Glen and [crew member] Bernie [Hallisky]. I've never had a Silver Crown car as close to perfect as that night."

A few laps later, Hewitt was tripped up in traffic and slid into the outside wall.

"A couple of laps later, I saw Jack parked up into the fence," said Stewart. "I just couldn't believe it. I radioed Glen and said, 'How many cars do we have to pass?' and he didn't answer. I screamed it again, and he yelled back that he was counting. Finally he came back and said, 'If you're in the top two, we've got the title.'

"We were fifth at the time, but on the restart [George] Snider and [Donnie] Beechler both got past. But I got back past George, and then I started picking off cars. I couldn't believe it. I had to do all my work in the corners with the V-6. We finally got up to Beechler, who was leading by then, and that's where we finished."

The scene in the Niebel pits was bedlam. Niebel and his co-owner, Willie Boles, were in the midst of pure, unabashed joy among crew members, fans, and friends.

"As soon as we slowed down [after the finish], I started calling to Glen on the radio," Stewart said. "But he had already ripped off the headset, and I pulled in there and it was very, very emotional. I'll never forget it, as long as I live."

He took the title by just two points.

That left just one more goal to attain: the USAC midget championship.

The early part of the season belonged to Danny Drinan, who had built a progressive new midget that was setting speed records everywhere it went. Drinan won at Phoenix in a blazing duel with Davey Hamilton that was marred by a spectacular crash at the finish.

Tony Stewart had his share of battles with Danny Drinan as well. At Richmond, Kentucky, on July 3, Drinan was leading the feature when Stewart dropped to the bottom of the track, taking the lead coming off turn two. At the other end, Stewart moved up on the banking. Drinan drove in under him, and there was contact. Stewart was parked, and Drinan went on to win the race. He was later fined $1,000 by USAC and lost his feature points.

At IRP one month later, Stewart led when Drinan attempted to pass both Stewart and the second-place car with one bold move in turns one and two. Drinan's car slid up into Stewart, who crashed into the outside wall and was done for the night. As an angry Stewart gestured, Drinan once again went on to win the race.

Shortly thereafter, Drinan was fined $1,000, lost 30 points and was suspended for two races.

"Before Richmond, Danny and I were fine," said Stewart of his arch rival Drinan. "I still respect him greatly as a fabricator and admire the fact that he can build such a great race car.

"But I think he's at a point in his life where he's trying to make things happen, and sometimes it's at others' expense. We talked later that night after the IRP deal, and he kept trying to justify the thing, and tell me why it was OK. I mean, I just don't respect that."

"Now [Drinan] is crying and moaning about how the world owes him something, ripping USAC, ripping me. It's ridiculous. He's just not willing to take responsibility for his own actions. You know, Billy Boat and I can race for thirty laps and bang each other ten times, and not worry about taking each other out. But [Drinan] crashed me twice within about a month."

While the suspension ended Drinan's chances for a championship, the two crashes put a hurt on Stewart's title hopes, too. He'd sagged to sixth, 85 points behind front-running Andy Michner. In fact, even after the lost points, Drinan remained 56 points ahead of Stewart.

At that point, East and Lewis became the cheerleaders.

"After Drinan took us out, Tony said that just killed us on the points," admitted East. "But I kept telling him, 'Let's just go on and see how it plays out.' "

Stewart and master chassis builder and wrench Bob East were a winning combination in midgets.
Jim Haines

By winning three open-wheel titles in one year, Tony Stewart became known as one of the top drivers in the sport— ever. *Randy Jones*

This was a bit of a role reversal. Earlier in the season, Stewart was the one preaching about points. "Tony is a good kid, and he was really good to work with," East said. "We knew he wanted all three titles, and we agreed that we'd work with him on managing any conflicts. And it turned out there was only one direct conflict."

A July sprint race at Wilmot, Wisconsin, was directly opposite an IRP midget race. Stewart elected to go to Wisconsin. While Johnny Parsons was winning the IRP race (Mike Bliss replaced Stewart for that event in the Lewis machine), rain was washing out Wilmot.

After the missed start and the two wrecks, Stewart got back on track. "He won and had a couple of seconds when we went to Kansas City," said East. "As soon as he got on that little roll, he was real easy to race with."

In the end, Stewart's midget season boiled down to a stretch run. Once again, he and his team stepped up. In September, Stewart met an early-season objective when he won the prestigious Hut Hundred at Terre Haute. Going into the event, Michner led Stewart by 41 points. But Michner broke early and dropped out. When the race was over, Stewart had sliced the lead to just seven points.

Stewart then won the midget feature at the Eldora Four Crown Nationals, fighting off Kenny Irwin Jr. in a splendid last-lap duel. He eventually ran a string of 10 straight races where he finished third or better and that was the strength he needed. The clincher came on Thanksgiving, when he finished seventh in the Turkey Night Grand Prix at Bakersfield, which was won by red hot Billy Boat.

Thanksgiving. A perfect day to make history.

"It was like a dream come true," Stewart said. "I don't think it will soak in for a while because now my name is on a list with some guys that I have admired, guys like Foyt, Vogler, and Pancho Carter. To be even mentioned with those people is an honor. I don't think I really understand it yet."

He's not alone.

"It's hard for people to understand the significance of this," said USAC news director Dick Jordan. "I would say it's one of the most incredible accomplishments in the history of racing. Three national open-wheel titles, in the same year, all running a full, complete schedule."

Consider these facts. In USAC's 40 years, only Pancho Carter has also won all three titles, and he did it from 1972 to 1978, with no two coming in the same year.

Only 18 drivers in USAC history have won multidivision championships; only 4 had previously won two in a single season: A. J. Foyt (championship and stock cars, 1979); Rich Vogler (sprints and midgets, 1980); Rick Hood (Silver Crown and sprints, 1985); and Steve Butler (Silver Crown and sprints, 1988).

The closest anyone had ever come to a triple was Vogler in 1980, when he finished third in the Silver Crown points, along with his two titles.

Over the past 40 years, only five USAC drivers have won more than four national titles. Period. Foyt has 11; Mel Kenyon and Vogler have 7 each; and Roger McCluskey and Butch Hartman have 5 each. Their ages when they clinched their fourth title? Foyt was 29, Hartman was 34, McCluskey was 40, and Kenyon's fourth came at the age of 41.

Stewart won his four titles at the age of 24.

"Even when Rich [Vogler] won two in 1980, nobody really ever thought someone could win three in one year," said Jordan. "It was neat to see a guy run all three series, but you never thought anyone would seriously challenge for all three, let alone win them all. It's something that might not ever be duplicated."

Now Stewart faces what he calls "the million-dollar question." Where does he go from here?

After the Sacramento race, he tested A. J. Foyt's Indy car at Phoenix. The test went very well, but it appeared at press time that Stewart wouldn't get the ride for the upcoming IRL season.

"Our [Phoenix] test was really good," said Stewart. "I learned a lot and it was really a different experience. A. J. was a lot of fun, and he was the most easy person you can imagine, easy to understand.

Left
Tony Stewart at Bakersfield on Thanksgiving Day, poised for an unprecedented USAC Triple Crown. *Mike Arthur*

Below
Stewart wheeling the Neibel/Bolles Silver Crown car at DuQuoin, on the way to the title in 1995. *Ken Coles*

"But it comes down to what is firm, and you have to go with a deal that you think is the most secure."

Stock cars offer that security. Stewart likely will run a limited Busch effort (18 to 20 races) next season with Harry Ranier, a former Winston Cup car owner, and a collection of Ranier's partners. It's a new team.

"I think it would be neat to run the Busch Series," said Stewart. "It is super competitive, and I think the experience will make me a better race driver. Sure, I'd still like to run Indy cars some day, and maybe I will. I'm still young. And I want to still race a few sprint cars and midgets. I love racing on dirt.

"They [the Busch team] realize that my heart is in open-wheel racing. I'm from Indiana, you know. I wouldn't run a lot of [open-wheel] races, but I'll run some select shows as long as it doesn't conflict. They're not crazy about that because with a million-dollar sponsor, they're worried about me getting hurt.

"I think if they are worried about me getting hurt, they shouldn't let me get out of bed in the morning!"

FREQUENT FLIER

Although the logistics for the triple crown of 1995 were challenging, no travel experience has been as daunting as a short haul from Springfield, Illinois, to Indianapolis in August 1993. Stewart friend and benefactor Larry Martz tells the story:

"Tony had made arrangements to run Ben Leyba's Silver Crown car Saturday afternoon on the mile at Springfield, Illinois, then make a quick trip to Indianapolis Raceway Park for the Pavement Nationals that night. He had talked with somebody about providing a plane, so we figured we could make the trip back to IRP in plenty of time. We drove to Springfield, and someone was going to take the car back for us, so all that was handled.

"Tony crashed early in the race, so we caught a ride to this little airport nearby. We hurried into the terminal, and a guy standing there was waiting, and he said, 'Are you Tony Stewart?' Tony said yes, and the guy explained that he was the pilot and would be flying us back to Indianapolis.

"We walked outside, and all these beautiful small planes were sitting out there, and we were walking along, looking at all of them and smiling. We kept going, and finally there was just one plane left, sitting out there all by itself. Tony and I looked at it, and looked at each other, with one of those looks like, 'No, it can't be . . .' But it was.

"This airplane was about a 1941 model military plane. It had one of those sliding canopies over the cockpit. The pilot had another guy with him, so we all squeezed into the airplane and he fired it up and we took off. It was so loud you couldn't hear yourself think, and we were flying along toward Indianapolis at about twelve miles per hour, I think. Finally, after some time had passed, the engine just quit.

"The pilot got the thing restarted, and it died again, then restarted, died. Did that several times. The pilot is rocking the wings back and forth, and he yells, 'I can't get my tanks to switch!' Tony and I were looking at each other with total fear in our eyes and I thought we were history. I mean, I've seen and done a lot of things, including duty in Vietnam, and this was the most scared that I've ever been.

"The pilot finally put the plane down in some abandoned airstrip in the middle of a cornfield. We couldn't raise anybody, and the pilot fiddled with the plane a little bit and got it restarted. Looking back now I can't believe it, but we actually got back in the plane and took off again. The pilot knew of an airstrip eighteen miles south where he could fix the plane.

"Well, we made it to the other airstrip, and finally flew on to Eagle Creek Airport near IRP, and caught a quick ride to the racetrack. We parked way out back, cut in front of everyone at the pit gate, and were running like maniacs around to the tunnel. They were qualifying, and by the time we got around to the main straight, we were exhausted and slowed to a walk. Rollie [Helmling, the car owner] saw us walking. He was really steamed and yelled across the track for us to quit lollygagging along and get moving. So we ran the rest of the way.

"We got to the pit and Mike Fedorcak was strapped in the car. Rollie yelled at Tony, 'You've got 30 seconds to get changed!' He made it, and he actually got a pretty good lap in. He wound up finishing sixth that night. That day was the most scared I've ever seen Tony, and the maddest I've ever seen Rollie!"

It probably marked the only flight in history from Springfield to Indianapolis with two stops. And no peanuts.

Stewart is determined to take it to the next level. But if he doesn't make it? "If I wound up just being a sprint car driver," he said, "there's nothing wrong with that."

His father tells the story of going to the IKF nationals in Iowa with a 12-year-old Tony Stewart. He knew Tony was a very determined kid and cautioned him about what they were about to see.

"We had a little trailer, and one kart, and one engine," said Nelson Stewart. "I told Tony that the other teams were gonna have big trailers, and lots of engines, spares, stuff like that. I told him to be realistic about how we would do on our first trip out there."

A few miles down the road, young Tony spoke up.

"Dad, we're gonna win this race."

"That's exactly what I like to hear," Nelson told his son.

A few years later, in the feature event, Tony beat defending nationals champion Mike Berg for the win. Berg's team indeed had multiple karts and multiple engines, but in the end, the talented Indiana kid simply beat everyone.

At the finish a very classy Berg removed the No. 1 sticker from the front of his kart and carefully placed it on the front of Stewart's machine.

And there it remains.

A Dangerous Crash

Stewart's high-flying early open-wheel days were sometimes just that as this four-page sequence of photos from a 1992 sprint car race at Salem, Indiana, will attest. Stewart (25) and Steve Butler (69) have nowhere to go in trying to avoid the spinning car of Mike Blake (81) on the narrow Salem high banks. While Butler and Stewart somehow manage to avoid Blake, Stewart can't keep his car off the tail of Butler's, launching his mount completely out of the ballpark while Butler takes a nasty tumble. Neither driver was injured in the incident, one that was sure to get the young Stewart's attention. *John Mahoney*

So, how to judge the inaugural Indy 200 at the Disney World Motor Speedway? Do you look at the first outing of the new Indy Racing League (IRL) with the optimism of its founder, Indianapolis Motor Speedway president Tony George, who deemed his new series "just what the doctor ordered" not 10 minutes after the checkered flag dropped?

Or do you look at this historic event through the eyes of those loyal to Championship Auto Racing Teams (CART), who promptly declared the Disney affair to be, well, a Mickey Mouse affair, contested largely by unknown drivers incapable of staging a competitive 200-mile Indy car race?

The answer is not to judge the race at all. Not yet, anyway. Five years from now, or 10, you will be able to look back and see the impact of this day very clearly. If the IRL becomes the success that Tony George believes it will be, those who were at Disney World on Saturday, January 27, 1996, will speak of the day with reverence, the way aging hippies fondly reminisce about Woodstock. And if the IRL is a bust, its first race will go down as just the opening chapter in a very sad motorsports story.

All you can say for sure in these first days after the engines went quiet in Orlando is that, as races go, the IRL opener wasn't the most exciting 200 miles of speed ever witnessed. What it was, really, was a dull race made memorable by a tight finish, Buzz Calkins edging Tony Stewart by 0.866 seconds at the flag. Not that this was anything new: The two closest finishes in the modern history of Indy car racing—the Indy 500 in 1992 and the Michigan 500 just last year [1995]—came at the end of lousy races, too.

But if the 200 itself was an artistic dud, the weekend was both a promotional hit and a spiritual home run. The joint was full, the entire three days had a big-event feel, and the IRL stood up on wobbly legs and, for the first time, walked. And open-wheel racing had changed forever.

Stewart and the Indy Racing League were both fresh faces on the motorsports scene at the start of the 1996 season at Orlando, Florida. *Dick Berggren*

Thursday

As soon as the first official practice sessions opened at the triangular new "Mickyard," it became apparent that this was not your average Indy car event. Right to the head of the speed charts shot names like Calkins, Stewart, Buddy Lazier, and Roberto Guerrero. Neither Calkins, fresh out of a hot-and-cold Indy Lights career, nor Stewart, a 1995 USAC champion in sprints, midgets, and Silver Crown cars, had ever competed in an Indy car event; Stewart, in fact, had never raced a rear-engined car. Lazier had been highly rated for years, but never managed to land a decent CART ride. And Guerrero's career has been in limbo ever since a 1987 testing crash at Indianapolis left him with serious head injuries.

Topping them all was another rookie, 1995 Toyota Atlantic champion Richie Hearn, who had come to the IRL with his title-winning Della Penna Motorsports team. Baby-faced but lead-footed, Hearn was obviously a quick study.

"The more I run these cars," he said, "it's almost like the speed feels slower and slower. I guess it's because your mind gets used to it, and you just react quicker."

Another fast learner was Stewart, who had shown up on race weekend having done just 65 Orlando test laps in his John Menard entry, plus some Phoenix hot laps in October in an A. J. Foyt car. Schooled on the toughest bullring tracks in the country, he admitted that the Disney layout was challenging but nothing extraordinary.

"Everybody keeps saying how spooky turn one looks," Stewart said, "and I'm thinking, 'If you think this place is spooky, try going wide open around Winchester in a midget.' "

The Menard's Racing Team proved to be a force right out of the box in the 1996 IRL season. Here, Stewart hits pit road for service at New Hampshire that season. *Bill Henry*

He was characteristically modest about his early speed, saying, "We're taking small steps, working at our own pace. We're not really worried about what everybody else is doing. We had a game plan before we came down here, and we're sticking to it. We'll get up to speed eventually. We're not real far off now."

No, he wasn't. When the day's last session ended with 24 cars having practiced, Stewart was fifth on the list, behind Hearn, Lazier, Guerrero, and Calkins.

A bit further back was supermodified superstar Davey Hamilton, joining Scott Sharp and Mike Groff in a three-car Foyt stable. Unlike Stewart, Hamilton had tested extensively at Disney—some 400 laps, he figured—and used his practice laps to get used to the traffic he expected to see during the race.

"Today is the first time I've run with a lot of other cars," Hamilton said, "and it's been very interesting. I'm pretty comfortable in the car by myself, but being out there with all the other guys is a whole new learning curve. You're trying to stay out of everybody's way, and at the same time you're trying to find the fast line."

Hamilton, who came close to making the 1995 Indianapolis 500 but missed when his car's undertray worked loose, called the Orlando track trickier than Indy. "Things seem to happen so much faster here," Hamilton said. "Our entry speed [in turn one] might be only 190, and at Indy you're going 230, but this is a sharper corner and you're on a much smaller track. You're just *busier* here."

It was drivers like Hearn, Stewart, and Hamilton—rookies from different disciplines of the sport—who were supposed to be scaring the daylights out of all sensible Indy car folks, if you listened to the anti-IRL rhetoric making the rounds all winter. But one of the most experienced racers on the Disney grounds, former Formula One driver and six-year CART vet Eddie Cheever, mocked such criticism.

"Who gave these comments?" Cheever bellowed. "Who said these things? Have they been here? Have they seen these guys drive? If they were here, or if they'd actually seen these guys drive, I'd be more than happy to listen to what they had to say."

Did Cheever think that, generally speaking, the IRL newcomers were OK? "Absolutely."

Another guy with plenty of experience, three-time Indianapolis 500 champ Johnny Rutherford, agreed. Granted, Rutherford now cashes a paycheck as the IRL's special projects coordinator, so it would be hard to call him impartial; on the other hand, he had been a strong advocate for the advancement of young American talent into Indy cars even while he was associated with CART as lead driver of that league's PPG pace cars.

Rutherford said, "Just because we don't have the Little Al Unsers or the Emerson Fittipaldis or the Bobby Rahals—the guys who are the so-called stars in CART—doesn't mean you're not going to see some great drivers here. This outfit is building its own stars. And I'll guarantee you, all some of these young drivers need is a little seat time, and any of those guys running over there [in CART] would have their hands full with 'em."

Friday

An amazing qualifying day crowd of 37,000 was still winding its way through Disney's maze of access roads, parking lots, and gates when Eliseo Salazar, a Chilean with a wide background in Formula One, sports cars, and Indy cars, interrupted an early practice session in a big way. Salazar's Dick Simon Lola brushed the third turn wall, careened into the pit wall, and then rocketed into the concrete barrier outside turn one. Just three days earlier, Salazar had said, "Twenty years from now, I can say I ran in the first [race] at Disney World." He spoke too soon. His injuries—including a fractured thigh bone and a gaping wound from a suspension piece that penetrated the car's tub and went through his leg—meant that if Salazar saw the green flag at all, it would be on a television set at the Orlando Regional Medical Center.

John Menard (second from right) assembled a potent IRL team in 1996 with drivers Scott Brayton, Tony Stewart, and Eddie Cheever.
James Compton

Three other IRL hopefuls would also watch this first Indy 200 from someplace other than the cockpit of a race car. They were Rick DeLorto, Jim Buick, and Bill Tempero, all denied opportunities to qualify by USAC officials after failing to post competitive practice speeds. It was a brave and commendable decision, given the already short field on hand. Coupled with Salazar's crash, it meant that only 20 cars would start the race.

The fastest of the bunch in qualifying, surprisingly, was not Richie Hearn. A fuel pick-up problem on both of his time-trial laps slowed the kid who had thus far been the star of the weekend. He ended up second, and the look on his face said plainly that second wasn't good enough. "Maybe I got a little spoiled because we went so good in practice," Hearn said, "but I really wanted the pole."

Which went instead to Hemelgarn's Buddy Lazier, at 181.388 miles per hour. For Lazier, who had watched the promising-young-driver phase of his career slip away and who, at age 28, was in danger of turning into a tail-end CART journeyman, it was a day of redemption. He admitted that accepting lesser rides in recent years "has been very difficult. But I take personal gratification out of knowing that I got the most out of what I've had to work with."

Lazier was asked if the frustration of being saddled with such cars had ever caused him to think about quitting. Very quietly, he said, "Absolutely."

If ever you needed justification for the existence of a second Indy car league, there it was, in Buddy Lazier's reply. He is a solid racer who, until Orlando in January 1996, had gotten precious few chances to drive solid cars and nearly gave it all up as a result.

While Stewart managed a second-place finish in the inaugural IRL event at Orlando, the highlight of the 1996 season was winning the pole position for the Indianapolis 500 that year. Here, Stewart (20) and fellow front-row starters Davy Jones (70) and Eliseo Salazar (7) power up as they head toward the green flag. *John Chilton*

His team owner, Ron Hemelgarn, has also known frustration. An off-and-on CART entrant, Hemelgarn was one of the first owners to support the IRL. He was sensitive to the knocks the new league had received prior to its first event. As he sat in the interview room beside his driver—with Hearn and second-row starters Roberto Guerrero and Arie Luyendyk also at the head table—Hemelgarn said, "I know there have been comments made about second-class car owners and second-class drivers [in the IRL], but I disagree. You look up at this table: These aren't second-class drivers. They're all true racers. And I don't look at myself as a second-class person. I'm very, very proud to be part of the IRL." The league, Hemelgarn announced, was here to stay. "You just have to look up in the stands," he said, "and you can see that this is real. This isn't something that's going to go away."

Luyendyk mentioned that in CART's 1991 Michigan 500, "I started 22nd and last. There were only 22 cars there. So I think we have a pretty good field for the first [IRL] race."

It was an upbeat, optimistic press conference, and most of the faces in the paddock area seemed happy once qualifying was out of the way. If only the day had ended right there.

Hearn and ninth-fastest qualifier Cheever were running hard in the final practice session, trying to find comfortable race setups, when they collided heading into turn one. Both cars ended up in the wall, with Cheever's Menard Lola crashing violently. "The other car was trying to pass me, and he touched the back of my car," Cheever told the print and electronic media folks who swarmed his team's transporter. A television guy tried to get in a question about Hearn's lack of Indy car

The eyes have it as
Tony Stewart awaits
an IRL practice run.
Herb Dodge

experience, but Cheever cut him off. "Racing is full of possible accidents," he said. "He probably thought he had more room than he did have, and we just touched wheels. I will be here tomorrow. Very angry, but I will be here."

Both teams opted to run backup cars in Saturday's race, Cheever's outfit rolling a fresh green Lola out of their trailer, and Hearn's Della Penna group borrowing a Reynard from Guerrero's Pagan Racing camp. That moved Hearn and Cheever to the back of the grid, leaving Lazier and Guerrero on the front row for the revised starting order, followed in the next three rows by Luyendyk and Scott Sharp, Calkins and Hamilton, and Stewart and Stan Wattles. Winning from any further back than that seemed all but impossible.

Just that quickly, two of the favorites had knocked themselves out of realistic contention in a practice crash. And practice, as wise ol' Johnny Rutherford was overheard to mutter, "doesn't pay a dime."

Saturday

At 8:40 on the morning of his big race, Tony George checked on how Hearn's team was coming with its borrowed car. Then he paused to discuss the way the event had gone so far.

"I feel really good," George said. "We've had a good weekend; a little bit more excitement than I would have liked to see, but still a good weekend. I'm proud of the guys who made the commitment to us and showed up here, and the fans clearly have enjoyed and supported what we've put on." As he spoke, 51,000 of those fans were in the process of filing into the track. George was asked if perhaps the arrival of this day would finally convince the world that, as Hemelgarn had proclaimed on Friday, the IRL was for real.

George paused a bit. Then he said, "I feel that anybody who has been looking at this thing with a jaundiced eye, looking at it critically, would certainly now have to think that this league has a lot of potential. I've always asked people to wait, to give us a chance, and not to prejudge us."

On his own, George brought up the CART/IRL stand-off: "Obviously, we had hoped to have a lot of the CART competitors come and run with us. That was our plan from the beginning, and we're sorry that they're not here. We think that they're missing a great opportunity." Maybe that last line was a dig, maybe it wasn't. Either way, Tony George, the single most important man in Indy car racing at the moment, did sound conciliatory when he added, "Hopefully, over time, things will work themselves out."One of George's top captains, USAC vice president Cary Agajanian, was also making the rounds on race morning. The weather forecast for the day included showers, and indeed there had been rain in the area on Friday night. Forget the rain, Agajanian said. He was listening to a higher authority. "Last night at about midnight or 12:30, after we finished our last meeting, I looked up at the sky," Agajanian said. "The clouds were breaking, and I saw some stars. And I thought back to my dad."

His eyes filled up as he spoke. His late father, J. C. Agajanian, won the Indianapolis 500 twice as a car owner, but across the 1950s and 1960s he was one of America's most colorful race promoters. Cary Agajanian said, "The night before a big race, he'd be nervous. Then he'd look up at the sky and say, 'Well, there's some stars. We're going to be OK tomorrow.' So I was looking up last night, and I said, 'Boy, this is just what my dad would do.' "

A. J. Foyt tells a wonderful story about how, when he was just a promising young driver from Texas in the late 1950s, J. C. Agajanian flew him out to California to compete in a midget race. "I'd never been on an airplane before," A. J. said. That trip was one of the biggest breaks in Foyt's early career. Now history was repeating itself. Had it not been for some heavy lobbying by Cary Agajanian on behalf of Tony Stewart—the closest thing USAC has these days to a young A. J. Foyt—Stewart would never have landed his ride with John Menard, and everything about this entire weekend would have been different. The IRL was supposed to help grass-roots American drivers like Stewart get the same shot at the big time that promoters like J. C. Agajanian once gave to Foyt, Parnelli Jones, or Troy Ruttman. If you understood all of that, you knew that Cary Agajanian's emotion on this day was due to more than just the weather.

Even though Stewart didn't have any experience driving Indy cars, he quickly became one of the top drivers in the IRL.

Stewart, meanwhile, was acting cautiously optimistic about his first Indy car start. "I'm still learning the car," he said. "It's hard for me to tell the guys exactly what needs to be done because I haven't driven these things enough. But we're sticking to our game plan. I think we'll be OK." He was more than OK when the green flag dropped; Stewart was sensational.

In fact, for the first quarter of the 200-lap race, he was the star. While Lazier built a small early lead over Luyendyk and Guerrero, Stewart went on the march. He passed Hamilton for sixth on lap seven; five laps later, he darted around Calkins for fifth; on lap 15, he moved to fourth, dispensing with Sharp. And then Stewart really went to work. He streaked past Guerrero for third on lap 18, just as a caution flag waved for Richie Hearn's long slide into the inside retaining wall out of turn one. ("Something broke," said Hearn's car owner, John Della Penna.) The yellow allowed Stewart to close on the leaders. He passed Luyendyk for second when the green flag reappeared on lap 24, stalked Lazier for a while, and then drove beneath him entering turn two. That was that. Tony Stewart was leading the first Indy car race of his life.

"I wasn't really pushing the car at all," Stewart said. "I was taking my time and being very, very careful. But everybody else just seemed to slow down and back up, so we just took advantage of it."

He had a theory about everybody else backing up: "We set the car up all weekend to have a lot of understeer. With me being a rookie, we felt it was safer to build the car with some understeer in it. And the longer we ran on the first load of fuel, the more the car became neutral."

The more experienced guys, he guessed, started out with neutral setups, only to have their cars get loose as they used fuel. Eventually, the same thing happened to Stewart, whose car was getting noticeably tail-happy by lap 50. "That was a totally new experience," he said. "I called in on the radio and told the guys we were starting to get loose, and that it felt a little bit on the uncomfortable side." They advised Stewart to back off, and he did, handing the lead on lap 66 to Calkins, another rookie who was smart enough to let things come to him.

"We'd had the luxury [in testing] to do long runs on full tanks," Calkins said. "That helped us set our car up. For the first ten or fifteen laps, the car really wasn't handling all that great, but then it came to me. My car didn't change, but it seemed like everybody else's cars started to drop back."Well, only some cars dropped back: Guerrero, Sharp, Hamilton, Robbie Buhl, ex-Ferrari Formula One shoe Michele Alboreto, and Menard drivers Cheever and Scott Brayton were all battling various handling problems. Other cars dropped out, notably pole sitter Lazier's with a bad right-front suspension link.

By halfway, only Calkins and Stewart remained on the lead lap. Pretty soon, they became the entire race. Luyendyk broke a gearbox, Brayton surrendered to his car's loose chassis, Hamilton had a suspension failure and then crashed while running a steady sixth, and everyone else slipped farther and farther behind these two rookies, Calkins and Stewart.

Calkins was going to win the thing going away until, just 11 laps from the end, Eddie Cheever had his second hard impact of the weekend when he and Sharp wrecked in turn one. Stewart, running second, said, "I was happy to see the yellow." But he wasn't happy for long. A pair of safety vehicles, speeding toward the crash site, "pulled right out in front of us," Stewart said. "Two trucks went out at the same time at two different spots on the racetrack, and it totally blocked the track. I was still in sixth gear, trying to catch up to the leader, and I had just started going down through the gears."

He slid up the track, ran through some debris, thumped the wall squarely with his right-front wheel, dove between the wreckers, dodged the crashed cars, and came out with his car in one piece. He doesn't know how. "I hit everything," Stewart said. "I hit debris; I hit the wall. The wrecker ran over my wing. I was steering every which direction the wheel would go, and I was cramming gears and brakes and bouncing off the wall. I'm really surprised we didn't get taken out of the race. We're lucky we didn't puncture a tire or hurt the suspension."

Stewart showed admirable courage but questionable judgment when he elected not to pit to check on the damages, a move that would have dropped him to the rear of the line on the restart. He preferred to stay directly behind Calkins because, Stewart said, "I felt like we had a good race car for the end."

As soon as the green waved for the final time on lap 194, he made one last serious bid to the outside of Calkins. But Stewart's car had picked up a push. "I didn't realize we had cracked the front wing [in the incident with the wrecker]," he said. "But I knew something had changed the handling of the car because we weren't near as strong as we were earlier. It got a lot of understeer toward the end, and that was because we'd cracked the wing."

And so Buzz Calkins won the Indy 200 at Disney World by less than a second. Two laps down were Buhl and Alboreto, third and fourth, respectively. Guerrero, who never lived up to his pre-race speed, was three laps down in fifth. "I'm kind of in shock that I'm sitting here," Calkins told the press corps, which was gracious enough not to admit any shock of its own. "This being my first Indy car race, I would have been happy with a top five."

In the Stewart camp, nobody wanted to take credit for their wonderful finish. The driver applauded crew chief Larry Curry: "Larry gave me a car that ran great all day." Curry, in turn, tipped his hat to car owner John Menard: "I called John and asked him about [hiring] Tony Stewart. He said, 'If you think it's the right thing to do, let's do it.' Without John's vote of confidence, Tony isn't driving the car." Menard, too, pointed fingers, saying, "We're terribly proud of Tony. He had all the poise of a veteran. It's easy to look back and say in hindsight, 'Gosh, we were smart for picking him.' But, you know, I'm very grateful that we did."

At the postrace press conference, it became apparent just how much a rookie—even on this day of rookies—Stewart really was. After third-place finisher Buhl told reporters how he had used his sway bar adjustment controls to adapt to changing track conditions, someone asked Stewart if he had done the same thing. He shook his head and replied sheepishly, "They just showed me this morning how to adjust the bars." And that wasn't all, Stewart said. "They asked on the radio one time, 'Can you cut the boost down?' and I said, 'Which button is the boost?' Then they said, 'Turn the [fuel] mixture up,' and I said, 'Where's the mixture [knob] at?'"

Robbie Buhl looked as astonished at Stewart's comments as the media folks did.

It seemed smart to give the last word of the day, of the weekend, really, to Tony George. Flushed with the success of his event, the IRL boss was happy to oblige. "I couldn't be more pleased," George said. "These guys certainly proved that they're professionals. They proved that they were never in over their heads. They were always under control." He nodded in the direction of Calkins, Stewart, and Buhl. "All three of these young guys deserved a shot, and that's what the IRL is all about. They got their shot, and they made the most of it." But alas, the best last word on the weekend came not from George, but from John Menard, who had enough faith in George's idea to haul three teams to Orlando. He, too, pointed to Calkins, Stewart, and Buhl and said something that might have sounded brash coming from Tony George, no matter how true it was. John Menard said, "I don't think any one of these three guys would have been in Indy car racing this year had the IRL not come along."

He was right. And open-wheel racing had changed forever. Wait a while, and we'll see how much.

The Graduates

STAFF REPORT
OPEN WHEEL, FEBRUARY 1998

Plenty of people know Tony Stewart, and plenty know Davey Hamilton, and with the two of them getting ready to decide the 1997 Indy Racing League championship, it seemed as if everyone in the garage area at the Las Vegas Motor Speedway wanted to pal around with one of them or the other. But nobody in the place knew them both better than Anthony Joseph Foyt, and thus it seemed wise to seek out the greatest racer this country has ever produced and ask him what he thought of these two young drivers.

And so here was Foyt, in the shadow of his team's transporter, kicking that around for a moment. He does not gladly suffer fools, or foolish questions; he can brush off a reporter as easily as he once brushed the dirt from his uniform after sprint car races at Ascot or Williams Grove. But he understood the significance of his connection to Hamilton and Stewart: He hired one of them and came damned close to hiring the other. It was aboard Foyt's car, after all, that Stewart cut his first Indy car laps during a Phoenix test in the autumn of 1995; it was a terrific audition, but the ride went to Hamilton, and Stewart later signed with Team Menard. Now they had all come to the 1997 season finale, Stewart and Menard leading Hamilton and Foyt by just 10 points in the IRL standings.

"They're both very good race drivers," Foyt said after a pause, "but they are a little bit different. What I mean is, they both run hard, but they do it in different ways. At the beginning of a race, Tony might charge a little bit more, where Davey will sit back and see what he's got. But it's not like Davey's conservative, because you'll see Davey hang it out when it comes right down to it.

"It's a tossup, really. They're both great race drivers."

There was no hiding Foyt's pride at seeing the IRL title up for grabs between two short-track graduates. Foyt himself had towed midgets out of his native Houston in the mid-1950s, graduating to sprinters throughout the Midwest and landing at the Indianapolis Motor Speedway—where he would win the 500 four times—in 1958. But across the 1970s and 1980s, as Indy cars evolved technically and began to race more on road courses and street circuits than traditional ovals, their owners began to see little value in a racing education like Foyt's; it became much more important that a driver come with plenty of rear-engine experience. And so CART, which grabbed control of Indy car racing from USAC at the dawn of the 1980s, became overrun by road racers, both domestic and foreign-born, their first laps cut not on the bullrings of Foyt's youth but at racing schools and in various amateur divisions. It did not hurt that, in general, the young road racers displayed more of a knack for arriving with sponsors in tow than their oval-track counterparts did.

It was a system Foyt claimed to hate, even as he occasionally caved in and hired the odd European or Mexican road racer himself. When the IRL, an all oval-track series, was launched by Indianapolis Motor Speedway president Tony George in 1996, Foyt committed immediately. He gave Stewart, fresh off his 1995 triple-crown season of USAC midget, sprint, and Silver Crown championships, that Phoenix test; then he signed Hamilton, a gifted star of the West Coast supermodified scene.

The 1997 IRL championship came down to a final one-race battle between Tony Stewart and Davey Hamilton. In the end, Hamilton finished 7th and Stewart 11th, still good enough to give Stewart the IRL title.
Ron McQueeney

"Davey and Tony both, they came up kinda the same way I did," Foyt said. "Now they're driving Indy cars because of their ability and not their pocketbooks. They learned by racing on the short tracks, and the biggest thing the short tracks teach you is quick reactions. They just sharpen you up and make you a good racer.

"I've set a lot of records and won races all over the world," Foyt said, "and it wasn't because I went to any driving school."

Nor did Stewart and Hamilton, unless you count the hard-knocks universities they attended for years on Friday, Saturday, and Sunday nights. Stewart studied at Terre Haute, Winchester, and Indianapolis Raceway Park, under professors named Hewitt and Sills, and Reeves; Hamilton was tutored by Rebel Jackson, Chuck Gurney, and his own father, Ken Hamilton, at Meridian, Phoenix, and Mesa Marin. They have been sneaking peeks at each other's homework for a long time.

"It's kinda like we've grown up together, even though we were from different places," Stewart said. "I definitely knew who he was because you'd pick up *National Speed Sport News* every week and read where Davey Hamilton won another supermodified race."

Hamilton said, "I'm sure we were both aware of each other. Tony was from the Midwest and I was a West Coast guy, but we'd meet in the middle at races like the Copper Classic at Phoenix. As a matter of fact, the first time I really noticed him was back in '93, when I won the pole for the Silver Crown race at Phoenix and Tony won the outside pole. From that point on, I paid attention to him."

They developed a casual friendship, which has deepened across the past couple of years, when they have been occasional teammates on the Silver Crown team fielded by George Snider. On the first day of practice for the Las Vegas 500, both used the same term—"good friends"—to describe their relationship.

"Is that going to make this weekend easier or harder for you?" Stewart was asked.

He said, "Both. It's easy, because I'm racing with a friend of mine. At the same time, it's also hard knowing that one of us isn't going to win it. But if we can't win it, I can't think of anyone I'd rather see win it than Davey."

The same question was put to Hamilton, and his answer was remarkably similar: "In a way, I'd rather go into this race fighting with a guy I didn't care about. That would make it easier. But you know, there's no one I'd rather lose to than Tony. I'm going to give it all I have to win this championship, but if I can't have it, it'll be good to see Tony get it."

Stewart's IRL championship run was benefited by the input of chief mechanic Bill Martin. Here, Stewart and Martin discuss ways to get more speed out of their Menard entry in the final race at Las Vegas.
Ron McQueeney

And both were emphatic about one point, articulated here by Stewart: "No matter what happens—whether Davey wins this title or I do—nothing is going to change between him and I."

They are, as friends tend to be, different people with different personalities. Around the racetrack, Stewart wears an all-business game face; Hamilton is more loose, at least outwardly. And yet while both seemed to agree with Foyt's opinion that Stewart generally charges harder than Hamilton does, they claimed that their driving styles were essentially pretty similar.

Listen to Hamilton: "Tony has led more laps in the IRL than me or anybody else, so I'm sure he's a little more aggressive than I am at times. But I think we've got a lot in common, too. We both seem to take care of our equipment—neither one of us crashes a lot—and we both respect other people on the racetrack."

Now hear Stewart: "Davey is a solid guy, a driver you can trust. He'll bring his race car home in one piece, and at the same time he'll get everything out of it. I'd like to think I'm the same way."

Each of them adapted handily to Indy cars. Stewart has been flashier, right from his Disney World debut with Menard in January 1996, but Hamilton has often been more effective. And they are both right in claiming to be kind to their cars; when you think about the wreck-strewn races that have peppered the IRL's short history, rarely do visions of Hamilton and Stewart come to mind. It was, in Hamilton's view, a matter of training.

"What you learn on the short tracks," he said, "is how to get a pass done cleanly. As close as we run in these IRL cars, you need to know how to race wheel-to-wheel. All year long—Charlotte, Texas, Colorado—we've been shooting it out in traffic. In that situation, the short-track experience that Tony and I have has definitely helped.

"We may not have a lot of Indy car experience, but we do have a lot of racing experience. I just wasn't sure in the beginning if our kind of experience was going to let us excel here; I thought Tony and I could do this, but I wasn't one hundred percent sure. But it has worked out pretty good for both of us."

As a matter of fact, it has worked out perfectly for fans of sprint cars, midgets, and super-modifieds. Stewart may have said it best: "No matter how this thing goes between Davey and I, somebody who grew up on the short tracks is going to win the championship."

It took no great leap of imagination to believe that after Las Vegas, things would get better still for those weekend warriors who harbor Indy car dreams. Already, the success of Stewart and Hamilton had helped usher into the IRL a couple of other short-track aces—Billy Boat as Hamilton's Foyt teammate and Jimmy Kite with the Scandia operation of Andy Evans.

"What me and Davey have done definitely didn't hurt Billy and Jimmy," Stewart said. He was happy about that, of course, because he will always be a midget and sprint car racer at heart. But Stewart also conceded that if this trend continues, he and Hamilton will have done themselves no long-term favors.

"It's going to make things tougher in the IRL," he said. "Trust me, I didn't mind missing some of those midget races in the last couple years because Billy Boat is tough to beat in those cars. Now he's tough in these things, too."

As if to prove Stewart right, Boat went out that Thursday night and won his first Indy car pole with a lap of 207.413 miles per hour around the 1.5-mile D-shaped track. The run ended what he called "a 24-hour roller coaster," and he wasn't kidding. In order, Boat practiced well in Foyt's Dallara, crashed, and then argued with Roberto Guerrero (nearly coming to blows), ran off the pace in a back-up g-force, and rebounded with a flat-out run in the repaired Dallara.

"The harder I pushed the car," Boat said, "the better it felt."

Stewart was also right in another respect: Boat sure was making things tough for his IRL foes, particularly his own teammate. Prior to Boat's run, Hamilton had been the top qualifier with a speed of 205.300, and the two points that the IRL awards for winning a pole would have narrowed Stewart's lead to eight.

The stress of battling for the 1997 IRL championship is clear in this shot of Stewart on pit road at Las Vegas. The concern proved to be justified as Stewart could only manage an 11th-place finish in the event. *Ron McQueeney*

Boat had drawn a spot near the end of the qualifying line but ahead of Stewart, who was due to run last but hadn't shown his usual blistering speed. Plenty of folks expected Foyt to pull Boat's car out of line, let Stewart run, and then react accordingly: If Stewart beat Hamilton's time, Foyt could send Boat on a banzai run in an effort to rob Stewart of the two points; if Stewart failed to top Hamilton, Foyt could simply instruct Boat to cut a good, safe lap.

Foyt, perhaps typically, left the mind games to others. He told Boat to stand on the gas, watched him knock off Hamilton, and then stood by as Stewart timed third at 205.113. Conventional wisdom was that A. J. had shot himself in the foot, and perhaps shot Hamilton in the ass. Even Stewart admitted to being surprised when Boat took the pole, saying, "I didn't honestly think Foyt would let him."

Hamilton, for his part, was in no mood for second-guessing. "My job is to drive the race car," he said. "Anything else is not my call."

The man who did make the call was more forthright. Foyt's emphatic defense of his decision dominated the post-qualifying press conference to the point where his drivers, flanking him on either side, were reduced to supporting actors. It all began when Foyt was quizzed about the wisdom of letting Boat run for the pole.

"I'm glad you asked that question," Foyt said calmly. Then he turned up the volume a bit, pointing out that he owed as much to Boat's sponsors as to Hamilton's ("They're paying me to represent 'em equally"), vowing that he would never ask one of his drivers to give way to another ("Like in Formula One, where they say the number one driver's going to run first, and then number two"), and making it crystal clear where the buck stopped on his team ("A. J. runs this operation"). It was Foyt at his bombastic, now-listen-here best, and you didn't necessarily need to agree with him to enjoy the show.

"I've won seven of these championships," Foyt declared, "and I never had nobody give me one. I'm damn sure not going to give it to one of my guys if he don't deserve it. If Davey runs good Saturday night, he'll damn sure have earned it, and I think that's the way he wants to win it, not [to have] some writers, down the line, say, 'Well, if it wouldn't have been for them two points Billy gave him, he wouldn't have been the champion.' I don't think Davey would want to win a championship that way."

Someone in the media throng was quick to prod Hamilton to respond. If they were looking to start trouble, Hamilton wasn't biting.

"I got hired to drive a race car for A. J.," he said, echoing his earlier line, "and that's what I do."

At another point in the press conference, however, he may have let a bit of frustration show through.

"If I win this championship," Hamilton said, "I'll guarantee you, I earned it."

How tightly wound were the principal players as the race drew near? On Saturday afternoon, with the start just hours away, John Menard was asked how he was feeling. Menard, who carries himself with the kind of confidence you expect in a self-made multimillionaire businessman, said, "I'm pretty really nervous at this point."

What he meant to say, of course, was "really pretty nervous," but it was easy to forgive Menard his slip. Prior to joining the IRL, he had entered cars in just one race each season, the Indianapolis 500, and he had gotten used to surviving just one high-pressure race morning each year. Now here he was at Las Vegas, on the heels of a successful 1997 campaign—with Stewart scoring in Colorado and Robbie Buhl winning at New Hampshire—sweating out a run for his first-ever series title.

Team manager Larry Curry and members of the Menards team stand guard over Tony Stewart and his IRL entry prior to qualifying for the final 1997 event at Las Vegas. *Jim Haines*

"I didn't realize how tough this was going to be," Menard said. "It's been a lot more pressure than I anticipated."

What added to the race-day pressure was a day-long wind with gusts reaching 50 miles per hour. Since the Las Vegas Motor Speedway is surrounded by desert some 15 miles outside the city for which it is named, it was clear that plenty of sand was riding in on all that wind and settling down on the track.

That was confirmed when IRL officials announced that the first three laps of the 500-kilometer (208-lap) race would run under yellow, in hopes that the circulating cars might clean the surface.

Stewart, two-wide at a Phoenix IRL event.
Frank B. Mormillo

Depending on who you asked, this well-intentioned move either helped a little or didn't help at all once the green flag waved. Whenever a car strayed higher than the second groove, its driver found himself struggling just to keep it away from the concrete wall.

One guy who had the track figured out was Jeff Ward, who bolted from the sixth row into the lead after just one green flag lap. At the other end of the spectrum were the two men with the most at stake; Hamilton was the first to start backsliding, and then Stewart began to drift backwards after briefly hovering in fourth and fifth.

The Menard and Foyt teams had calculated that Stewart needed to finish ninth or better to clinch the crown if Hamilton won. By the time they had run 25 laps, all that math went out the window because the chance of either man winning looked dim.

Stewart said, "At the beginning of the race, I thought we had a pretty good night going because Davey was backing up. Then our car started pushing."

Which meant that in their race-within-a-race, the two championship contenders had opposite problems because Hamilton's car was, in his words, "way loose. I don't know if it was the wind, or what, but the car was very loose right from the start."

Little by little, their battle for superiority dissolved into a contest to see who would be less inferior. In the biggest Indy car race of their careers to date, Tony Stewart and Davey Hamilton became bit players. In fact, if you simply checked the scoreboard every so often to see where they were running—example: at lap 70, Stewart and Hamilton were 13th and 14th—you might have figured them for two strokers out to merely collect points. But if you watched their cars carefully enough to grasp their handling woes, you would have understood exactly how hard the pair was working.

Each had at least one very visible brush with disaster. On lap 96, Stewart came so close to the wall exiting turn two that the radio broadcasters announced he had smacked it. Stewart himself was not sure: "I don't know if I hit it or not. I was puckered up so tight [that] I don't think I'd have known if I did hit it."

And on lap 114, Hamilton slid dangerously high in turn three, gathered the car up nicely, and then repeated the maneuver when he reached turn one. He said, "I got into turn three a little too hot, just trying to take the car to the limit, and it got loose. I had to drive up the track to keep from spinning, which put me in the marbles. Then I went down into turn one and, because I had all that rubber on my tires, I did it again. I was lucky I didn't get into the wall."

So it went. While others looked brilliant—Ward was a rocket until being knocked from contention by a pit road speeding violation, Mark Dismore was stunningly quick, Scott Goodyear was a rocket late in the going, Buhl was fast and steady, and Eliseo Salazar rode the best car of the night all the way to victory lane—Stewart and Hamilton each drove with one eye on his points rival and the other on whichever portion of the wall he seemed about to slide into.

Stewart said, "I felt like I was in a Silver Crown race on the mile at Springfield." Right feeling, perhaps, but wrong analogy. In a Silver Crown race, he would have been a lot closer to the front.

When the checkered flag waved, Hamilton was a lap down in 7th, with Stewart three laps farther back in 11th. That left Stewart six points ahead, and earned him the 1997 Indy Racing League championship. His reaction, after a tired grin, was this: "It wasn't pretty, but we got the job done."

He admitted to being mystified by his handling problem—"Maybe a shock went away or something, because we just could never get the push out of the car"—and was clearly happy just to climb out of the thing.

Somebody said, "How many real serious scares did you have?"

"Probably a dozen," Stewart said. "There were so many times I almost hit the wall. You could have used a feeler gauge to see how close we were sometimes. I thought, 'Is this race ever going to end?'"

Stewart embraced his team manager, Larry Curry, a veteran of 22 Indy car seasons who had toiled on several teams in various capacities before joining Menard prior to the 1994 season.

"This is absolutely the biggest moment of my career," said Curry. "Not only had I never won a championship, but I hadn't ever been with a team that was in the hunt for one. Winning a race is great, but it's something you did right on a particular day; a championship is something you do over an entire season."

His boss, John Menard, who had been so jittery heading into the race, found that the title had cured his nervousness.

Stewart's dreams of winning an Indy car championship are captured in his smile as he poses with the 1997 IRL championship trophy. *Jim Haines*

"I'm going to sleep just fine tonight," he said, beaming. "After I have a couple beers."

A few hundred yards away from the delirious Team Menard, Davey Hamilton sat alone on the pit wall and tried to look on the bright side.

"We didn't give up tonight," he said. "We kept plugging away at it, and we got the car fast at the very end of the race. It was just a little bit too late."

Was it too soon for Hamilton to put this result behind him and look back at his season?

"No. We had a good year, a year I'm proud of. We finished more laps than anybody else, which is a tribute to this entire team, and we did what we had to do to put ourselves in a position to win this championship. But Tony did what he had to do, too, and he won it.

"I guess," Hamilton said with a shrug, "this is the way God meant it to be."

When Stewart met the media an hour or so after the race, he turned the event into a celebration of his roots. He made repeated references to sprint cars and midgets and proclaimed that the IRL had only begun to dip its toe into the short-track talent pool.

"There's a lot of guys like me out there, and they're just waiting," Stewart said. "A lot of them aren't necessarily ready now, but they will be in two or three years."

He recounted his first exposure to his Menard teammates, which occurred early in January 1997 after USAC's Cary Agajanian had arranged an Orlando test a few weeks prior to the IRL opener.

"It was like going to a foreign land," Stewart recalled. "I didn't know anybody, didn't know anything."

With the pressure of the championship chase off, Stewart and Menard share a laugh in victory lane after winning the 1997 IRL title at Las Vegas. *Jim Haines*

Today he is a champion, not to mention one of the most exciting Indy car drivers to emerge in the last half-dozen years. It was fairly common to hear IRL-bashers brush off Stewart's early success by suggesting that his competition wasn't very stiff, but he has taken the measure of an impressive list of drivers who came in with years of experience in high-speed, rear-engined cars: Goodyear, Guerrero, Salazar, Buhl, Dismore, Arie Luyendyk, Eddie Cheever, Richie Hearn, Davy Jones, Buddy Lazier, Mike Groff, John Paul Jr., Vincenzo Sospiri, Michele Alboreto, Johnny O'Connell, Scott Sharp. There are a lot of CART miles (Formula One miles too) represented on that list.

It was inevitable, then, that the reporters in the Vegas press room would end up asking Stewart where he thought his career might have been had the Indy Racing League not come along. He answered that he would likely be pursuing a career in NASCAR, since "there weren't any opportunities" for short-track racers in CART. "I don't think anybody in CART even knew who I was," Stewart said.

It seemed appropriate to ask IRL founder Tony George, who stood in a corner of the room as Stewart spoke, if he felt vindicated by the season-long showings of Stewart, Hamilton, and the league's other short-track graduates. But George, not much on grandstanding, said the credit belonged not to him but to the drivers themselves.

"They got their shot," George said. "They got their opportunities, and they did very well, and that's all that matters. Young guys like Davey and Tony are going to be our future."

Still, the whole thing warmed the hearts of many an old short-track hand, including IRL pace car driver Johnny Rutherford, who in his racing days busted out of the bullrings and rode his ability all the way to three Indianapolis 500 wins.

"This isn't a closed shop for sprint and midget drivers," said Rutherford, "but seeing these young men get this chance, and seeing them show everyone what they can do—show that they're racers—has been gratifying to me. It has been like a breath of fresh air."

But let us give the last Las Vegas word to Foyt, who knew the subject better than anybody in the joint. An hour after the race, he stood quietly and watched Hamilton's crew stow its equipment for the long ride back to Houston.

The term "good loser," Foyt has said, was as ridiculous to him as "jumbo shrimp." Still, by his standard, Foyt was gracious after this defeat.

"You're going to win a few, and you're going to lose a few," he said. "I knew the only way we could win was if Tony had bad luck and Davey had good luck."

Foyt sighed. "I guess we just weren't championship material this time."

He was asked if he felt some degree of pride for Stewart, given their shared heritage.

"Well, I'm not happy about losing to him," Foyt said, going instantly to his standard defensive answer. He looked for a moment like he would leave it at that. But then, perhaps understanding that this had been no ordinary loss, that Indy car racing was once again something he could relate to, he smiled just the tiniest bit.

"Tony deserves this," Foyt said. "He's a true champion."

The Jump to Stock Cars

Stewart made his NASCAR Busch Series debut in 1996 running nine events that season. Pictured here in the No. 15 Ranier Walsh Pontiac, Stewart appeared to be headed to Winston Cup in 1997 behind the wheel of a Ford, but those plans, as we now know, got short-circuited. *Brian Spurlock*

Tony Stewart's rise through and success in the open-wheel ranks quickly drew the attention of car owners everywhere. That was especially true in the area surrounding Charlotte, North Carolina, home to most of the teams that compete in NASCAR.

After all, hadn't some of NASCAR's brightest stars come from the open-wheel ranks? Tim Richmond made the jump to NASCAR superstardom in the 1980s and NASCAR phenom Jeff Gordon took the same open-wheel route to the top of the NASCAR standings in the 1990s.

With team owners frantically searching for "the next Jeff Gordon," Stewart seemed a likely choice. Young, fearless, articulate, and already famous for becoming the first driver to ever win the USAC "Triple Crown" in 1995, Stewart appeared to have all the right credentials to jump to NASCAR. The fact that Indy car racing had fractured with the split between Championship Auto Racing Teams (CART) and the IRL also had Stewart casting an eye to the south and NASCAR as well.

Stewart's introduction to the world of NASCAR racing would prove to be bumpier than a 10-inch rut in the third turn at Eldora. Stewart made his NASCAR Busch Series debut on March 30, 1996, in the Goody's 250 at Bristol Motor Speedway piloting the No. 15 Ranier Walsh Pontiac to a 7th-place qualifying effort and a 16th-place finish.

In all, Stewart competed in nine 1996 NASCAR Busch Series events, never cracking the top 10. In 1997, Stewart concentrated on the IRL, winning the division championship. The title chase left little time for NASCAR as Stewart competed in just five races, posting a career-best third at Charlotte in the All Pro Bumper to Bumper 300 in October.

Despite the less than stellar results behind the wheel of a stock car, Stewart had shown more than enough to catch the eye of a number of car owners, sponsors, and manufacturers. It didn't take long for the bidding process to begin.

Stewart made his NASCAR Busch Series debut at Bristol, Tennessee, in the No. 15 Vision 3 Pontiac in 1996. *Brian Spurlock*

Stewart Comes to NASCAR

BY BRUCE MARTIN
CIRCLE TRACK, FEBRUARY 1997

Tony Stewart wants to win the Indianapolis 500. Tony Stewart also wants to win the Daytona 500. Tony Stewart wants to be the star driver of the Indy Racing League. Tony Stewart also wants to be a star in NASCAR Winston Cup.

Tony wants to do it all.

What Tony Stewart wants to become is the A. J. Foyt of the 1990s, a race driver just as capable of winning in a NASCAR Winston Cup stock car as a high-tech Indy car. And because Stewart has displayed such dynamic diversity in his racing career, he is in high demand by both the IRL and NASCAR Winston Cup.

"Ever since I was little, I carry the same dreams all the way until now," Stewart commented. "I've always wanted to win the Daytona 500. I've always wanted to win the Indianapolis 500. I've always wanted to win the Knoxville Nationals. I've wanted to win the Chili Bowl. I've wanted to do it all. I've tried to be the Deion Sanders of auto racing; I've tried to do everything. As long as I can do everything, that is what I will continue to do."

Stewart displayed his ability to drive a variety of different racing machines when he became the first driver in history to win the USAC midget, sprint, and Silver Crown titles in 1995. That accomplishment earned the young driver from Rushville, Indiana, as much attention in NASCAR as it did in Indy cars. Now there is a tussle for his talents.

In 1996, Stewart became the poster boy of the IRL and generated as much publicity in the league created by Indianapolis Motor Speedway president Tony George as any other driver in the series. He started on the pole for the 80th Indianapolis 500 on May 26, 1996, and led 44 of the first 54 laps before his Menard V-6 engine quit and knocked the driver out of the race on lap 82. The next week, the 25-year-old Stewart was back on the Busch Grand National series battling his competitors at Dover, Delaware.

Stock Car Choice

In September 1996, Ranier/Walsh Racing announced that, with the help of the Ford Motor Company, the team and Stewart were leaving Busch Grand National and would move to the NASCAR Winston Cup in 1997.

"With Tony, I think he should be running the cars that he is going to be in permanently," Ranier said. "We would rather have a poor Winston Cup year than a banner Busch year to get him started. One thing I have learned by dealing with race drivers over the years—and dealing with good race drivers—is that good race drivers can drive anything, and Tony Stewart is certainly an excellent race driver.

"My son Lorin and I actually spotted Tony driving the USAC Silver Crown cars. We had vowed that we would not come back into Winston Cup racing until we had someone we could build a program around, and we felt that Tony, as adaptable as he is, would attract the type of people it would take."

Stewart's initial love of racing was in open-wheel cars like his IRL mount shown here. Still, he claims to have been on a path to NASCAR even before he drove his first IRL race in 1996. *Brian Spurlock*

Stewart would eventually wind up in Joe Gibbs' No. 44 NASCAR Busch Series entry in 1998, but only after some significant wrangling by the NFL coach and race team owner. *Harold Hinson*

Which series will Stewart decide best suits his talents? That is a question the young driver probably can't answer.

"If you ask Tony Stewart what he likes to drive, he is going to tell you whatever he is driving on that day," manager of Team Menard Larry Curry said. "He is a real racer. Tony's best performances have come in the Indy car. It is all going to come down to what he really wants to do. But there is going to come a point in time where Tony is going to have to really focus in on whether he is going to drive Indy cars all the time or he is going to drive stock cars all the time. He is going to have to pick a road and commit to it.

"For certain, there is no question that Tony Stewart is important to the IRL," Curry remarked. "But I don't think Tony Stewart's career—if he decides to go run Winston Cup—I don't think we can pull our tent down and say the IRL is over with. We have to move along. But yes, Tony Stewart is an important part of the Indy Racing League."

Ford Pull

Lee Morse of the Ford Motor Company was instrumental in putting Stewart behind the wheel of a Ford Thunderbird in Winston Cup racing. Ranier/Walsh Racing fielded Pontiacs in Busch Grand National and had plans on moving up to Winston Cup with Pontiac, but Ford was able to woo Stewart away from the General Motors manufacturer.

"Tony has been pretty impressive in everything he has gotten in and driven," Morse said. "True, most of it has been open wheel, but he has had some pretty glowing Busch starts. He isn't going to start out by qualifying on the pole and winning the Daytona 500, but I think he can make most of the races and get a lot of good experience in his first year in Winston Cup."

Stewart has indicated the plan to go into NASCAR Winston Cup was implemented long before he had a ride in the IRL. "Right now, I am contracted for the next three Indy Racing League races, but we didn't know that we would be running a full Winston Cup schedule next year," Stewart said. "So we are working with Harry Ranier and John Menard, and all three of us are trying to sit down and work to

Stewart gave up a dazzling career in open-wheel racing to concentrate on NASCAR. His competitive fire can be seen here as he peeks out over the cowl of his 1997 IRL entry at Charlotte, North Carolina. *Harold Hinson*

where we can get the schedule to work the best we can. I'm sure we will be at the Indianapolis 500 next year.

"There are definitely more opportunities in a stock car, plus there aren't enough races for me in the IRL right now. It's just a lifelong dream to be in stock cars. Not that it hasn't been a lot of fun being in Indy cars, too. But the opportunities were kind of shut down in Indy cars until this year, and I had already started a plan of how I wanted to get to Winston Cup racing. The IRL came along after all those plans were already in motion.

"I wasn't going to alter my plans and deviate from them to make the IRL work 100 percent. We did what we could to make it work last year [1996], and we'll do what we can to make it work the best we can this year [1997], but I just felt like the opportunities were better in stock cars right now."

Although Stewart was always in a position to win the IRL races he competed in, including the Indianapolis 500, his learning curve in Busch Grand National was a little more steep. *Mark Robertson*

IRL Poster Boy

Stewart has a tremendous opportunity in the IRL and admits winning the Indianapolis 500 is his lifelong dream. And Tony George had a driver like Tony Stewart in mind when he started the IRL—a series dedicated to promoting grass-roots, oval-track, open-wheel race drivers to the Indianapolis 500.

"There is no question Tony is a very talented driver," George said. "I've compared him to the likes of Mario Andretti and A. J. Foyt and Al Unser Jr. They are the kind of guys who can drive anything. They can be competitive in just about any car they have. Tony Stewart is aggressive, he is a competitor, and he loves to drive. He is young right now, he has a lot of enthusiasm and a lot of stamina. He gets out there and works. In the morning, he is thinking about it, and at the end of the day when he goes to bed, he is thinking about how to improve himself. In my conversations with Tony, I see a lot of the driver that is required to be the best.

"Talent is talent no matter how you cut it, and the kid has talent," George said. "I've seen him mature a lot in the last year and I think that has done more than anything to bring him into his own. He has a world of talent and is probably going to use it to the best of his natural ability in many forms of racing. We are happy to have him involved in

Waddell Wilson, who now runs the engine department for Darrell Waltrip's NASCAR Winston Cup team, worked with Stewart in Busch Grand National when he was with Ranier's team at the beginning of the 1996 season. Wilson-prepared engines have won seven Daytona 500s, and he has worked with such drivers as Fireball Roberts, Fred Lorenzen, David Pearson, Buddy Baker, Benny Parsons, Mario Andretti, A. J. Foyt, Lenny Pond, Bobby Allison, Cale Yarborough, Darrell Waltrip, and Ricky Craven. His stock car career began in 1963.

"The biggest thing is, Tony reminds me of Cale Yarborough," Wilson said. "He could come in and tell you what the car was doing, without knowing how to fix it, which was good. He could pinpoint what the car was doing because he has a great feel for a race car. Plus, the boy has nerves of steel. He is as brave as Dick Tracy. Most of those boys who come out of open-wheel cars have the bravery in these Winston Cup cars. They feel secure and safe, but very few of them can adapt to them. Jeff Gordon could and so can Tony Stewart. Those cars are easy to drive compared to these cars. You can't expect him to have an understanding of a stock car because he is not accustomed to working around them. But he can tell you what the car is doing so you can work on it."

Wilson cautions, however, that even with all of Stewart's talents behind the wheel of a race car, he is going to need equipment capable of putting him up front before his talent can become evident. "You have to look at what is behind him and what all is being done for him," Wilson said. "You have to look at the car he is in and the equipment. It doesn't surprise me he is coming to Winston Cup. Now, it is going to be up to how good the race car is going to be they put under him and the people who are there to teach him. Look at what Ray Evernham has taught Jeff Gordon. Tony is only to be as good as the car they put under him. He can complement what they give him, but it still takes great equipment for his talent to shine. I wish the kid the best because he is good."

the IRL right now, but there are a lot of other guys out there just like him who need the opportunity, and we expect to provide it.

"Attitude is everything and there are a lot of young guys out there with a good attitude like Tony Stewart. He is a racer; there is no doubt about it. He is a racer who needed a break and he got a break. I think the Menard/Stewart package could be something that is a contender for many years to come."

Indy vs. Stocks

Although Stewart has been in a position to win every IRL race held so far, including the Indianapolis 500, his learning curve in Busch Grand National has been difficult. Still, he hasn't backed away from the challenge. "As far as doing both, I don't think it is that hard," Stewart said. "I'm used to running 100 races a year; and to go from running 100 to 25, that can't be too difficult. But I have to go through two different learning curves, and I'm doing them simultaneously.

"A race car is a race car is a race car," Stewart said. "They all have four wheels. They have a steering wheel, a brake pedal, a gas pedal, and a clutch. It is not rocket science. They are all based on basics, and the people who get away from the basics are the ones who get themselves in trouble.

"I have fun in anything I drive," Stewart added. "I still run go karts every now and then just to get back to where I started. Anything that runs over 200 miles an hour is going to be a fun car to drive. I think everything I drive, I have fun with. Indy cars are a real joy. I love how fast we run in them, more so than anything else because these are the fastest cars we run.

"When you go from the Indy car to the stock car you have to remember you don't have ground-effects and you don't have wings. The big thing you notice off the bat is you aren't dealing with a 1,600- or 1,700-pound Indy car, you are dealing with a 3,300-pound stock car that has hard, skinny tires and no brakes, and a real sluggish motor. It takes some time to get acclimated again.

"I think all the training that I've done with USAC in the midget and sprint cars in the past, and jumping around between the three divisions, has helped me become versatile enough that when I get in the car I know it is going to be different and I know what it should feel like when I go out and take my time."

Overall, Stewart made the transition from the open-wheel ranks to stock cars look easy when he apprenticed for one year in the NASCAR Busch Series and then stepped up to the Winston Cup division in the Joe Gibbs–owned Home Depot entry. Here, his crew cracks off a quick pit stop at Daytona. *Sam Sharpe*

Stewart had his eye on stock car racing and the racing fraternity had its eyes on him. He is shown here in his Shell NBS uniform in early 1998. *Mark Robertson*

Stewart finds the challenges between the two vastly different types of cars unique. "Coming from the midgets and sprint cars, I'm used to running wheel to wheel with guys," Stewart said. "You don't see as much of that with Indy car racing. You go into stock car racing and you see more of that than you do in the midget and sprint cars. I like running wheel to wheel with the other competitors. There is a lot of thinking involved in running those cars. You can't just go out there and run 30 hard laps because you will burn your tires up real fast. There is a lot of thought in saving your equipment and being patient, and being in the right place at the right time. I think that is the biggest thing I like about racing stock cars.

"The thing that has fascinated me the most about Indy car racing is the technical side of it, how technical everything is and how one-thousandth of an inch here and there can really make a difference. I think a lot of people we work with have made it very enjoyable. They have challenged my mind more than anything.

"To do these two different series and go back and forth, both sides have challenged my mind to learn, and learn a lot in a short period of time. That is about the biggest thing that I have liked about this."

Foyt Review

That sounds just like a racing legend from an earlier era named A. J. Foyt, who could beat NASCAR's best with the same attitude it took to become the first four-time winner of the Indianapolis 500. "I really think if he gets in the right operation in NASCAR, Tony Stewart is a very versatile driver and can do very well," Foyt said. "I think the experience he has had out of midgets and sprints and Silver Crown cars will help him. It's just like Jeff Gordon; with the right opportunity, Tony Stewart can fly. Right now, he has had some bad breaks over there, but at least he has showed he can run over there in NASCAR.

"To me, Jeff Gordon ran midgets and sprints and he could run Indy cars, and is a very talented young driver and a good driver. I think Tony has the same quality Jeff Gordon does, but he has to have the right operation over there."

If Stewart eventually decides to stick with the IRL, Foyt believes it won't be long before he becomes a legendary name at the Indianapolis 500. "If Tony Stewart would be fortunate enough, which he is very capable of doing, and wins at the Indianapolis 500, he will go down with a name as big as Al Unser Jr. and Michael Andretti right out of the box," Foyt said. "Tony Stewart will overshadow them. He has already set a record for winning the Silver Crown, sprint, and midget titles in one year. He is going to go down as a great champion.

"Tony Stewart is going back to the old style of race car drivers: 'Let me at them. I want to race them and beat them at their own field.' He wants to race. He wants to show the world how good he is. Jeff Gordon could do the same thing—show the world they are race drivers and can drive every type of car. These kind of boys are few and far between, so you hate to lose them out of any series. Tony will have to pick which series he will be in, but let's face it, he is going to be big where he goes."

To hear praise like that from one of his racing heroes makes Stewart feel proud. "When I think of A. J. Foyt, I think of the greatest race car driver of all time," Stewart said. "If you look at what he has done, he has driven everything he could drive. I think there is something to that, the more experience you get. Any time you get in a race car, you are going to be better. Any time you can run a race, you are better off. He has run everything he could get into and gained a lot of knowledge doing that. I feel I've done the same thing and I've had the same theories he has; it is just a different era. I guess I am the A. J. Foyt of the 1990s, right now."

JUST HOW GOOD?

What makes Tony Stewart such a promising driver? He has yet to win an IRL event or a NASCAR Busch Grand National race and is ready to attempt a full NASCAR Winston Cup schedule in 1997. Those who know Stewart best—IRL team owner John Menard and team manager Larry Curry— believe Stewart possesses the unique blend of natural ability with an understanding of a race car chassis.

"I think Tony has a good feel for the car," said Menard, who has had such drivers as Formula One world champion Nelson Piquet and four-time Indianapolis 500 winner Al Unser Sr. drive his cars in the Indianapolis 500. "I think he thinks about the car a lot. When Tony gets up in the morning, he starts thinking about the car. He thinks about it all day long and he thinks about it at night. He is one of these guys who is not easily distracted by a lot of other things in his life. Perhaps, some of the older drivers have a lot more going on in their lives. Tony basically races.

"The other thing that makes Tony good is that he races all the time. He is running three nights a week, four nights a week in all kinds of different cars. He races and races. For the fun of it, Tony's idea of a good time is to go over to the go kart track when this is all done and go race go karts."

While some drivers bring their helmet to the racetrack and don't understand the car, others have total understanding of the vehicle they are racing. "I would say Tony falls somewhere in between," Menard said. "Tony has a good feeling for what has to happen in the car, but on the other hand, he doesn't try to be an engineer. He is just about the right balance that you want that way.

"He is very level-headed on the racetrack. He is like Al Unser Sr., perhaps. He is very calm and very deliberate. On the radio, that is how he comes across. Perhaps he is not as calm as Al Unser, but he is approaching that."

While Menard is the owner of the team, team manager Larry Curry not only calls the shots for Stewart's car but he is also the car's engineer. That takes a special level of communication between the driver and crew to prepare an Indy car that runs up front—something Stewart did in every IRL race in 1996. "Tony has a great feel for the race car," Curry said. "He has great car control. I think that comes from his racing a lot. Now, what we have introduced him to is the data age where he gets the information from the telemetry. He is getting used to seeing that now and relating that to what he feels in the car. I think that has helped him even become a little better.

"He is still trying to learn the chassis. Tony does not give us a lot of input that says we need to stiffen up the springs, or change the toe, or this or that. His information about what the car is doing and at what part of the corner it is doing it is very good."

Does Stewart have the ability to set the pace without abusing the car? "Absolutely," Curry said. "I've heard all the stories about why did Team Menard go out and run so hard at Indy? Why did Team Menard run so hard at Phoenix? Why did Team Menard run so hard at Loudon? Team Menard was not running that hard. I can't speak for why everyone else was not on the pace. Tony was not abusing the car. He was taking care of his equipment, he was taking care of the motor, and circumstances caught up to them. Yes, he can do that.

"He is also very level-headed. When you talk to him on the radio, he is very cool. He has talked to me before when he has been in traffic in the middle of three or four guys going through a corner, and he's on the radio talking to me. I'm like, 'Concentrate on what you are doing.' He is concentrating on what he is doing, but he is used to racing in a lot of traffic."

So how much of Tony Stewart's ability is hard work and how much is talent? "First of all, you have to have the talent," Curry said. "How do you measure that? How do you measure somebody's desire or whatever? Certainly, how he has developed his talent has been by getting in race cars and racing a lot

The Recruitment of Tony Stewart

By Bruce Martin
Stock Car Racing, July 1999

At the professional level (and sometimes in college, although it is illegal), coaches will use money, gifts, and other financial incentives to lure a talented free agent player in hopes of making their team a championship contender.

Joe Gibbs was a master of recruiting as an assistant football coach at San Diego State University. He earned a reputation as a tremendous recruiter by bringing outstanding high school talent to the Aztecs. Those same tactics paid off when Gibbs became the head football coach of the National Football League's Washington Redskins.

Gibbs often relied on free agent talent to keep his Redskins on a championship path. He had the ability to add just the right player to a team of winners.

Gibbs uses the same tactics today as a NASCAR Winston Cup team owner, and it has helped him land a race driver who has already proven to be not only a star of the future, but a star of the present—Tony Stewart.

The Courtship Begins

Joe Gibbs' recruitment of Tony Stewart actually began in 1996 when Stewart was gaining national attention in the first year of the Indy Racing League. As a driver for Team Menard, Stewart displayed a driving ability matching speed with smoothness. During that season, Stewart was also attempting to break into NASCAR by running a limited number of Busch Series races for an unsponsored team owned by Harry Ranier.

What Gibbs saw was the look of a winner, and he made a determined effort to lure Stewart to his NASCAR team. So Gibbs started to recruit Stewart, just as he would a football player.

"It was exactly the same, really," Gibbs recalled. "He had an existing contract, which had not gone well, and some things had fallen through on that. I had to go and work out a resolution with the people on that side. At the same time, I was talking to Tony and trying to persuade him that this was the right place for him to come. Of course, that's a big decision for those guys.

"I chased back and forth, across the country for about a month. Jimmy Makar, Bobby Labonte, and all of us sat and talked and concluded Tony Stewart would be the right guy to be a teammate for Bobby. That being decided, it was my job to get it done. That's what we did. We took off to get it done."

Because Gibbs had been a winner before in football, he had an uncanny ability to notice winning attributes in a professional athlete. He saw those qualities in Stewart.

"I liked his attitude," Gibbs said of the young driver from Rushville, Indiana. "He's not an ego guy. He talks to you about wanting to make the right steps in his career and not jump into Winston Cup when he isn't ready. I loved his attitude and willingness to learn. I thought he was the right person to represent us and the corporations—Home Depot and the other sponsors. I thought he was very talented."

Before wooing Stewart to join his team, Joe Gibbs spirited Bobby Labonte away from the Bill Davis Ford in 1995. Labonte, the 1992 NASCAR Busch Series champion, immediately paid dividends winning his first Winston Cup race just 11 races into the association when he captured the 1995 Coca-Cola 600 at Charlotte. *Paul Melhado*

Laying the Groundwork

So what were the tactics that worked so well for Gibbs in football that he was able to translate into NASCAR?

"I think persistence: letting him know how much you appreciate him," said Gibbs. "We would wake him up in the morning to let him know we were interested and how important he was to us. Obviously, there is always a financial part in this, too.

"I think in all of those ways, we were trying to get him to take a look at our organization and the people in it. He had a chance to visit with Jimmy Makar and Bobby Labonte. They were a part of the recruiting process. Generally, you are trying to sell somebody to stake their career on your organization.

"This probably applies more to a free agent in the NFL because money is legal. In college, it isn't. I think it is very similar to free agency in the NFL."

In the IRL, Stewart was running for one of the premier teams in Indy car racing—Team Menard. But in the NASCAR Busch Series in 1996, he was running with an operation that just didn't have the horsepower. In the NFL, the best teams often find that one special player on a losing team and give him the opportunity to play for a winner.

"The difference with Tony is that it wasn't just open-wheel racing. I think the year before we signed him, he raced 164 races," Gibbs said. "He raced everything from high-horsepower midgets to Busch Grand National racing for Harry Ranier. That wasn't a well-funded deal and the equipment wasn't great. It was his versatility and the fact he had been in a lot of big horsepower stuff, not just open-wheel racing. As a matter of fact, that was a small part of what he had done."

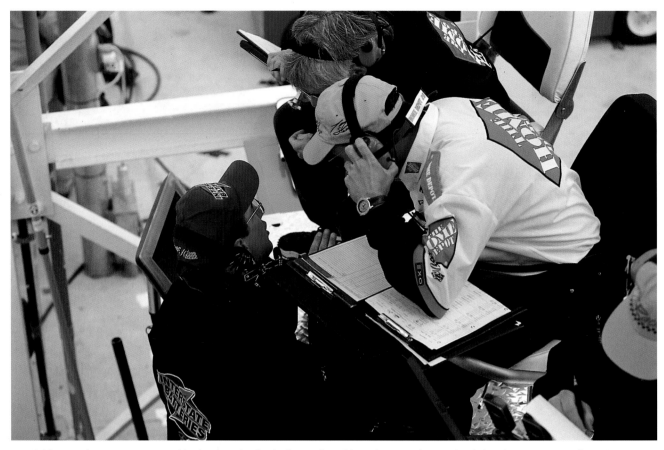

Joe Gibbs runs his race teams just like he does his football squads, tabbing key members to lead the charge. Here, Labonte's crew chief Jimmy Makar discusses strategy with Stewart's top kick, Greg Zipadelli. *Paul Melhado*

Ironically, when Gibbs recruited him, Stewart was not at the top of his game. It was one year after he had become the first race driver in history to win three major national championships in the same season. Stewart won the USAC midget, sprint, and Silver Crown titles in 1995. At the end of that year, he tested an Indy car for team owner A. J. Foyt, but had already signed a deal with Ranier to compete in the Busch Series with advancement into Winston Cup in 1997.

At that time, Indianapolis Motor Speedway president Tony George was engaged in a battle with CART over the creation of the Indy Racing League. Stewart exemplified all the qualities George was looking for as an IRL driver—a talented, American grassroots driver with an open-wheel, oval-track background.

Starved for talent in the IRL, Cary Agajanian—Stewart's lawyer and the former promoter of the now-defunct Ascot Speedway in southern California —lured Stewart to the IRL by convincing team owner John Menard to give the young Hoosier a chance. Menard originally wanted to put Jim Crawford behind the wheel of his Indy car, but relented and chose Stewart.

In his very first Indy car race, Stewart was a hit. He finished second to Buzz Calkins in the first-ever IRL race—the 1996 Indy 200 at Walt Disney World. He was the second-fastest qualifier for the Indianapolis 500, but started on the pole because of the death of pole winner Scott Brayton, Stewart's teammate at Team Menard.

Stewart went on to set a record for "most laps led at the start of an Indianapolis 500 by a rookie" in 1996 before dropping out with engine failure.

He was now the "Poster Boy of the Indy Racing League." Gibbs wanted to make him NASCAR's number one draft pick.

Phone Call . . . Again

Ironically, it took Stewart being sidelined with an injury during a Las Vegas IRL race before Gibbs could start his recruiting effort.

"The thing about Joe is that we talked while I was recuperating from the Las Vegas crash in 1996," Stewart recalled. "I was at my mother's in Indiana. I don't know how he found the number there, but he called and asked if I was happy with my deal or what my situation was with Ranier. At that time, we were still OK with everything.

"We went to Phoenix the next year. And I was with Team Menard in the IRL, and I got another phone call at the hotel. It was Joe Gibbs again. I thought, 'How is this guy finding me?' He found me in places I didn't think he could find me. At that point I was ready to make a change.

"From that day on, he called me every day like clockwork. He would call me from six to eight in the morning to midnight to two in the morning to make sure he got ahold of me each day.

"He was very persistent and worked really hard to make sure I had an open line of communication and didn't get away from him."

A Determined Gibbs

To have Joe Gibbs chasing after football players is one thing, but Gibbs has displayed his determination in NASCAR Winston Cup racing as well. He won the 1993 Daytona 500 in just his second season as a team owner. Dale Jarrett was the driver. The team was a consistent winner with Jarrett behind the wheel. When Jarrett left to join Robert Yates, Gibbs hired Bobby Labonte, a combination that has been one of NASCAR's best with Labonte near the top of [the 1999] Winston Cup title chase.

So when Gibbs called, naturally, Stewart listened.

"It was impressive, the guy was that persistent," Stewart said. "A lot of car owners would either expect you to call them or whatever the case. But Joe was very persistent. I'd get home late at night and I would get a call from Joe: 'Hey, is everything all right? How are we doing?' He was always checking up on me to make sure I was all right. He was that persistent. The fact that he cared that much about what was going on in my life is what made the difference to me.

"We just talked a lot. We built a relationship on the phone and through meetings where I got to see him. Nobody was going to sign me because of glitz and glamour. That isn't what it was all about. I did some of that with the IRL. I was strictly worried about performance and he was the same way, so we had a common interest and common goals."

By being on the receiving end of Gibbs' recruitment efforts, Stewart understood the qualities that put the coach into the Pro Football Hall of Fame.

"The way he pursued me, you could tell how intense he was," Stewart said. "You don't become successful without that intensity. He didn't have a big ego. He didn't say, 'Hey, I'm Joe Gibbs. You aren't going to be anything unless you go with me.' He was more like, 'Hey, we would really like the opportunity to work with you. We think you would be a great addition to our program. We think we can put a good package together.' He treated me like an equal, not like I was below him or above him, but like a person. You can tell how that would make a guy successful in life and as a football coach."

It didn't take long for Gibbs to win over Stewart, who quickly signed up on the winning team.

"Probably the third or fourth phone call at six in the morning or at two in the morning is when he won me over," Stewart remembered. "I was impressed with the fact that he was willing to do whatever it took to get hold of me. It was at that point where I said this is the opportunity that the IRL has been waiting for—a guy with this much persistence and who is dedicated to make sure I'm part of his program. This is the type of guy I want to work for.

"On the IRL side, I didn't have a relationship with John Menard because I didn't want a relationship. John Menard was out for John Menard. The nice thing about being with Joe Gibbs is Joe looks out for everybody. When one wins, we all win.

By the end of Stewart's Winston Cup rookie season, he was out front winning three events and two pole positions. Here, he leads another former open-wheel ace, Jeff Gordon. *Sam Sharpe*

"It makes you proud to be part of the guy's organization. When I show up at the racetrack, I'm proud to wear a Joe Gibbs racing jacket. I'm proud to wear my Home Depot colors, and I'm proud to say that I drive for Joe Gibbs. That is the kind of opportunity I was looking for because that is the kind of program I wanted to be involved in."

Stock Car Lessons

Stewart honed his craft as a stock car driver with a year in the Busch Series driving Labonte's Shell Pontiac. Although Dale Earnhardt Jr. and Matt Kenseth garnered most of the attention as the new stars of racing, Stewart quietly learned his lessons while splitting time between the IRL and NASCAR.

By the time Stewart arrived at Daytona International Speedway for the Daytona 500, however, his talent was obvious. He was on the pole until Jeff Gordon knocked him off as the next-to-last driver to make a qualifying effort. Stewart started on the front row of his very first NASCAR Winston Cup race, which happened to be Winston Cup's biggest race of all.

Stewart realized rookies do not have friends in the biggest race of the year, a race that is so dependent on a drafting partner. But rather than complain, Stewart learned. After qualifying well at Rockingham, Stewart qualified third at Atlanta in March. He scored back-to-back sixth-place finishes in the TranSouth Financial Services 400 at Darlington, South Carolina, and the Primestar 500 at Texas Motor Speedway.

Part of Stewart's growth curve was to share information with his veteran teammate, Bobby Labonte. At right, Stewart mirrors Labonte's No. 18 Gibbs' entry as they race through a corner. Below, the two get their laps in at the 2004 Daytona 500. *Nigel Kinrade*

Stewart really showed his promise at the Food City 500 at Bristol Motor Speedway where he qualified fourth, led a Winston Cup race for the first time, and dominated along with Rusty Wallace. But when Jerry Nadeau spun in the third turn, it caused a chain reaction crash that involved Stewart and Gordon. Stewart was two-laps down and unable to win the race, but he proved he was closing in on his first Winston Cup win.

Undaunted, Stewart bounced back the very next week to win the pole, his first-ever as a Winston Cup driver, at Martinsville.

Rather than take the credit, Stewart has been the team player—another key trait to a Gibbs' winning team.

"Tony has a great feel for a race car and that's important," Labonte said. "He's a rookie in Winston Cup, but he's not a rookie to racing. I think he's got a great feel for a race car and knows what the car is doing when he's right on. I'm sure the more experience he gets will probably work out better for both of us.

Above and right
Stewart's early NASCAR Busch Series effort didn't have the horsepower needed to be competitive. That's not a problem for Stewart and his Joe Gibbs Racing Home Depot entry. *Nigel Kinrade*

"He listens very well. He knows that he's in this thing as a rookie. At the same time, he's listening and observing and watching. From what I've seen, it looks like he's doing everything right. As far as me being a veteran, I haven't been around very long either, but there are things I've learned and if I can teach him so he doesn't have to go through the same learning curve I did, I will. I think he's very observant of what goes on the racetrack and with the race cars."

When Stewart has a question, he asks Labonte. But he makes sure he doesn't become a burden to his more experienced teammate.

"I don't ask Bobby to be my best friend, and I don't ask Bobby to take time out of his schedule," Stewart said. "Every second that I have time to talk to him is precious time. I try not to bother him any more than I absolutely have to. The good thing about Bobby is that he doesn't mess around. When I ask a question and want to know an answer, he gives it to me point blank and doesn't screw around with it. He tells me the honest answer and does it in a way that is no nonsense. I know what he is saying when he tells me things and he gets right to the point about it.

"I think when Greg Zipadelli [Stewart's crew chief] and Jimmy Makar [Labonte's crew chief] talk, it's more technical than anything. When Bobby and I talk, it's about where I need to be on the racetrack, how far to stay in the throttle in the corner, and how much brake we are using. The questions are different, but we are all looking for speed and lap times. We do share a lot. It's not a deal where we share some information, but we don't share other information. We share everything together.

"We feel like the purpose in having a two-car team is to use the other team to learn from, and use both programs equally.

Joe Gibbs earned a spot in the Pro Football Hall of Fame by being able to evaluate top talent as it came through the college ranks. Gibbs used those same skills to tab Tony Stewart for his NASCAR team efforts. *Doug Miller*

"Being a rookie in the series, I'm not sure I can help him much, but he is certainly helping me."

Recruiting new talent to make the team a winner doesn't always work in other sports. Adding a high-priced free agent often creates animosity on a team and can become very divisive. Gibbs has experienced that in football and wanted to make sure it didn't happen in NASCAR.

"You're never quite sure when you add somebody how the chemistry is going to work," Gibbs said. "They [Bobby and Tony] are just getting started. I think where you see two-car team help is when you see all the information. Obviously, Tony has more tests because he's a rookie. When he goes somewhere and tests, the information comes back, and it's something else for Jimmy to think about and sift through. There's another crew chief there for Jimmy to talk to now. We're still in the infant stages of building that two-car relationship. We're trying to do it a little differently. We're trying to keep everybody in the same shop. They all work side by side here, and we're trying to develop that kind of chemistry."

In a sense, Stewart arrives in Winston Cup the way the number one draft pick arrives in the NBA or the NFL. But Stewart is his own harshest critic and isn't prepared to live off his expectations.

Any success he has this season, Stewart believes, is from being on a winning team. And, as Gibbs proved with the Redskins, winning is often done by formulating a game plan.

"I'm not sure I'm progressing that much," Stewart said. "The team and the people I'm surrounded with are the kind of people that should be in a position we are in. We are very focused on our goals. We have stuck to our game plan, and, so far, have met every goal. As long as we keep doing that, I'm going to be happy."

Unless something unforeseen happens, Stewart is well on his way to winning the NASCAR Winston Cup Rookie of the Year. That will be another indicator of Gibbs' eye for talent.

"I think if you are a good recruiter, you will be good no matter where you are, whether it's the NFL or NASCAR," Gibbs said. "I really believe that. I picture myself, because of football, being more in a people field. In a people field, a lot is sales.

"I think people that are good coaches are good salesmen. That's how I look at it."

And so far, Gibbs' ability as a recruiter has never looked better, as is evident with his latest star, Tony Stewart.

Tony Stewart

Just Another Rookie . . . or the Greatest Thing Since Sliced Bread?

By Bob Myers
Stock Car Racing, July 1999

As a past champion in midgets, sprints, Silver Crown, and the1997 Indy Racing League, Tony Stewart, a self-proclaimed "14-year-old kid in a 27-year-old body," has been touted as the next coming of Jeff Gordon. Now in 1999, Stewart gets his chance in Winston Cup with the second team formed by Joe Gibbs Racing. Stock Car Racing's Bob Myers talked candidly with Stewart about his new team, goals, and very high expectations.

Why did you make a career shift to stock cars after much success in open wheels?

In all honesty, I've been interested in stock cars since day one. NASCAR was always where I wanted to be. I signed a NASCAR Busch Series deal with [car owner] Harry Ranier, but that didn't work too well. About the same time, Tony George was forming the Indy Racing League, and I decided to race there, signing a contract with [car owner] John Menard. All that happened within two weeks [in late 1995]. I didn't really care what I was driving. I just wanted it to be competitive.

What happened to the Ranier deal?

It wasn't sponsorship, as has been reported. Harry wanted to go to Winston Cup quicker than I did. I didn't want to hold him back. I didn't want to make a move until I felt I was ready. I had worked 17 years of my life to get to that point, and I didn't want to ruin my career with a bad decision.

How and when did you get hooked up with car owner and former NFL Coach Joe Gibbs?

He called me in the fall of 1996 and asked if I was happy with my arrangements with Ranier and if I had any plans to make changes. I told him I was pretty happy. During the winter, things changed, and I talked with him again in March 1997. From that point, we started putting a deal together.

Are you an NFL fan?

I shouldn't say no because I'll probably get in trouble. Really, I'm so concerned about racing that I haven't paid a whole lot of attention [to other sports]. Being from Indiana, I do try to follow the Indianapolis Colts some. I was more interested in baseball when I was growing up because I wasn't big enough [he's 5 foot, 9 inches, 160 pounds now] to think of football.

Considering it was your decision to start with Gibbs in the Busch Series, was it wise?

I think so, and I don't think it would hurt me to run another year in Busch. I think having Bobby Labonte as my teammate in Winston Cup will help me get through the learning curve a little quicker. That should take some of the question marks out of my mind about what we're doing and how we're doing it.

Are you generally pleased with your experience in Busch last year?

Oh, yeah, I don't think I'd trade it for anything. The Busch Series is very tough in itself, and you're racing with Winston Cup drivers on many weekends. What I learned definitely will help in Winston Cup.

Stewart models his new stock car duds—a NASCAR Busch Series uniform—in 1998. *Nigel Kinrade*

Last season, you had five top fives, including seconds at Rockingham and New Hampshire, in 22 Busch starts and finished 21st in points. Did you have a shot at a win?

Yes, I did. At Rockingham I was leading coming off the final turn on the last lap, and Matt Kenseth got by me. I'm not sure we had a chance at Loudon without a yellow. The thing that was exciting about the year was that we ran up front a lot, even though, at the end of the day, the results didn't show up on paper.

In terms of competition, how severe is the jump from Busch to Winston Cup?

Well, the competition is going to be a lot tougher in Winston Cup. But racing against Mark Martin, Jeff Burton, Jimmy Spencer, and other Winston Cup guys gave me an idea of what to expect. Running with them in Busch gave me hope that I can compete at the highest level.

Do you think familiarity with several Winston Cup tracks from Busch and the IRL will be an asset to you?

Definitely. Obviously, you don't have to learn them again. You hear drivers and crew chiefs talk about the first half of the season for a rookie driver as totally different than the second half. That is, I should be better the second time around. Knowing some tracks also will enable me to concentrate more on running the car.

Ready for the Big Time

Are you ready for Winston Cup?

I don't think you ever feel ready. I'd feel better about it if I had won two or three Busch races.

Do you know your first-year crew chief, Greg Zipadelli, former chassis expert for Jeff Burton at Roush Racing, very well?

No, but in the time we have spent together, we communicate and get along well. Our backgrounds are different, but we're die-hard racers who live the sport, and that's a good base to start from.

Have you communicated with Bobby Labonte?

We've talked some, and we plan to talk a lot more during tests over the winter. In the time we have talked, I've learned a lot and gotten a lot of information in a very short time.

How do you feel about driving Pontiacs in Winston Cup?

The Pontiac people keep striving to make changes that will improve the car. Their involvement in Busch was great. I think their dedication to the program is what I admire most about driving a Pontiac. They've been great to us, always asking what they can do for us.

Stewart had a lot of guidance in his first year with the Joe Gibbs Racing team. Here, he talks race strategy with crew chief Jimmy Makar and teammate Bobby Labonte. *Harold Hinson*

Stewart saw racing against Cup drivers in the Busch Series as a positive experience. Having a Cup-level crew, like the one on the No. 44 Shell Pontiac, helped too. *Jim Cooling*

What will be the hardest for you to learn?

I think to pace myself in the longer races. I've only finished one 500-mile race, at Indy in 1997. I think racing a stock car for three or four hours probably will be the biggest transition for me.

On what size tracks do you feel most comfortable and which will need the most work?

I run best on 1¼- to 1½-mile tracks for some reason. The superspeedways [Daytona and Talladega] require a different style with the restrictor plates. I'll really need to work on the short tracks, and the road courses will be my biggest challenge because I haven't run a stock car there.

Describe your driving style.

I learned how to be smooth by driving midget and sprint cars. I'm learning to be patient. In the IRL last season, it didn't matter whether I ran wide open or took it easy, we still blew. If your stock car is working well, you should take care of it. You don't necessarily have to lead. Mark Martin told me the race doesn't mean anything until after the final pit stop. We'll just try to stay in the lead pack and make adjustments on the car—until it's time to go.

Have you raced against Winston Cup phenom Jeff Gordon?

Other than the IROC Series, only once. That was an indoor midget race in Indianapolis. We never did get close to each other. He was in front and spun and had to pit. I got ahead of him and then dropped out with a mechanical problem.

Do you think you'll be as good as he is?

Well, I hope to be better. If we can have half the success he's had, it would be great, but I don't want to settle for that. I want to be the best. So do 42 other guys.

Is what Gordon has accomplished so quickly an incentive to you?

Sure, all the drivers know it can be done, not just me. It's a matter of finding the right chemistry and right combination. I look at what he's done as a positive example that shows what can be done.

Do you have a hero in racing?

I admire [Dale] Earnhardt. I've been watching him drive since I was little. I liked him when everybody booed him for winning so many races and championships. Just watching how he came through the field reminds me of the way I was in midget and sprint cars. Also, A. J. Foyt and Jack Hewitt [a veteran open-wheel driver] are good friends.

What are your realistic expectations for 1999?

It's most important to gain as much experience as possible, to complete every lap I can. As a rookie, I'm not worried about winning races. I'm going in with the hope of winning a race, but Winston Cup is strong and competitive. There are some good drivers who don't have a career win. I have to be realistic, given all the experience some drivers have. Hopefully, in the second year we can try to win races.

As a highly touted, blue-chip driver, do you think the expectations of Gibbs, your team, and fans will be too high?

I don't think so. Joe is a realist too, and he knows it will take time. The whole point of adding a second team is to try to help Bobby Labonte. I hope I can learn enough early so I can start helping Bobby and the No. 18 car before the end of the year.

Stewart learned many lessons in his first NASCAR Cup season. Above, Dale Earnhardt (3) shows him how to pass on the high side in a pre-race practice at Richmond, Virginia. *Rusty Husband*

How do you feel about having a big company like Home Depot—which operates 690 home-improvement stores in the United States, Canada, and Chile and is in Winston Cup for the first time—as your primary sponsor?

It's great. I've met with some of the people, and they're absolutely enthusiastic about getting into Winston Cup. And that's exciting for me. They're new to the sport, as I am, and we'll try to learn and grow together.

Will Home Depot expect too much the first year?

I've already had that talk with them [he laughs]. I've stressed that this isn't going to be easy—you just don't go in there and buy wins. They understand that it's a learning curve, and they're willing to stand behind me and allow me to take the necessary time to get in position to win races for them.

Why do you think Robby Gordon's attempt at Winston Cup was brief and unsuccessful?

I really don't know. I don't think Robby went to Winston Cup with the right attitude. I think he thought he was going to kick rear ends right off the bat. That's the wrong attitude, and it's certainly not mine. You have to get along with the people you're racing with 34 weeks a year. So far, I feel like I've been halfway accepted in NASCAR. A lot of the guys have been friendly and have helped me already. As a rookie, that's made me feel good.

In 1995, you became the first and only driver to win the USAC Triple Crown—midgets, sprints, and Silver Crowns—in the same year. Qualifying for the 1996 Indianapolis 500, you sat on the pole with the fastest lap—235.837 miles per hour—ever turned by a rookie and were named top rookie in spite of a DNF. In 1997, you won the IRL championship with Team Menard. What's your biggest thrill in racing?

We have run in so many series that it's hard to pinpoint one thing. My whole career has been a thrill. But winning the USAC Triple Crown and the IRL championship were two of the biggest.

Do you have any idea how many feature races you have won?

I'd estimate 270, including about 200 in go karts, 35 in USAC, and 3 in the IRL.

Was there a major career break for you on the way up?

One of my biggest breaks was when I moved from three-quarter midgets to full midgets in USAC. That was done through a friend, [IRL driver] Mark Dismore. I drove go karts for Mark and his father for five years, and Mark helped me get my first full midget ride.

When did you start racing?

At age eight in go karts. My father, Nelson, raced before I was born—go karts, dirt short-track stocks, and sports cars. I got interested through him, and he helped me a lot.

Where did you grow up—in Rushville, Indiana, your hometown of about 6,000 located southeast of Indianapolis, or in Columbus, a city of about 35,000 where you have a residence south of Indy?

I lived in Rushville, Indiana, for only one and a half years, and the family moved to Columbus. I claim Rushville not only because I was born there, but because the whole town supported what I was doing. That's why I support the town. It's sort of the home track for three-quarter midgets, and that's a big deal in town. When I started racing there, I was driving USAC midgets and sprints, and I became something of a celebrity because I was driving the bigger cars. Columbus is sports-oriented, especially the fierce rivalry of the two high schools. That's mostly what you saw in the sports pages at the time. I'm becoming well known in Columbus, but it's taking a while.

Living about an hour from Indianapolis Motor Speedway, did you attend the Indianapolis 500 as a youth?

I did go to the race three or four years, first when I was four or five years old and to practice and time trials more often. I didn't go every year, but a lot for practice and time trials. I watched the races on TV so I could see more.

By August of his rookie season, Stewart was comfortable behind the wheel of his No. 20 racer. That was especially true when he returned to his roots, the Indianapolis Motor Speedway, for the 1999 Brickyard 400. *Worth Canoy*

By the end of his 1999 rookie season, Stewart was back to winning races. Here, he celebrates a Cup win at Phoenix in November. *Kristin Block*

Do you enjoy mixing with fans?

I love it. When I was running sprint cars, I was one of the last to leave the racetrack. I stayed as long as there were people there. The fans are what make racing great. It's getting harder nowadays in Busch, IRL, and Winston Cup, and you don't get the time with the fans. That's the only bad thing about being in higher forms of racing. The fans are what it's all about. I used to do a lot of testing of IRL cars at Indianapolis Motor Speedway, and it was no fun because the stands were empty. When you go there to race in front of all those people, the place comes to life.

Will you continue to race in the Indianapolis 500?

Actually, Joe was the one who has made it possible to do that. Joe supports the fact that I've always wanted to win the Indy 500. It's the only IRL race I plan to run, and I don't know for how long, but at least in 1999.

What are your goals in Winston Cup?

I want to win a Winston Cup championship just like everyone else, but I think you have to look at it as a long-term goal. I think the speed and time frame (three years) that Jeff Gordon did it in is amazing. It would be hard to do it that quickly. It's a matter of my learning with the right people. I don't want to sit there and get a time frame on my mind on how long it's going to take to do that. I might never be able to win a championship. I'm always going to strive for it each year, and I'd love to do it seven or eight times.

A Rookie Report

A Look Back at Daytona

By Tony Stewart
Circle Track, July 1999

Stewart was cool, calm, and collected as he waited to make his first-ever start in the Daytona 500 in February 1999.

When you work for two-plus years to arrive at a certain place in your life, expectations are many times not closely related to how reality unfolds. Now that I had reached my goal of becoming a full-time NASCAR Winston Cup driver, I wondered what the future would hold as I arrived at Daytona International Speedway as an official candidate for the 1999 NASCAR Winston Cup Rookie of the Year.

I could not ask for a more perfect situation in which to go to Winston Cup than with Joe Gibbs as a team owner, the Home Depot as a sponsor, Greg Zipadelli as a crew chief, and Bobby Labonte as a teammate. We have set realistic goals for our season—to qualify for every race, run as many laps as we can, improve with each event, and win the Rookie of the Year title.

But the level of competition in Cup is intense, and the Daytona 500 is the biggest race of the season. We just had to take it one step at a time and stick to our game plan. The first thing on the agenda was to get our qualifying setup in place.

As we rolled out for practice the first time in our brand-new, bright-orange Home Depot No. 20 Pontiac, the reality of where I was and what the task was in front of me kind of hit me between the eyes. It was a little overwhelming but very exciting and exhilarating.

We practiced consistently with how we had tested, and I began to develop a comfort level with the preparations we were making for qualifying. We felt like we were going to have a good enough run to put us in the field, even if we had a problem in the 125 race.

It is hard to describe the emotions I felt as I walked to the car to make my qualifying attempt. I kept telling myself it was just another race and to do what I had always done when I got in the car. Joe and Greg gave me their best advice and offered their support before I buckled in to attempt to make not only my first Winston Cup race, but the biggest race I had ever run in my career.

I felt like the lap was pretty good, but I didn't believe the time my crew guy gave me over the radio as I drove around on my cool-down lap. When I headed into turn

Stewart burst on the NASCAR Winston Cup scene in a hurry, qualifying second for his first-ever Daytona 500. The vision of Stewart and his No. 20 Home Depot car at high speed have become familiar to race fans worldwide since that 1999 debut. *Paul Melhado*

four, the crowd was on its feet cheering and waving stuff, and I began to wonder if the time they told me was correct. It was. With less than one-third of the cars left to make their qualifying attempts, we were on the pole for the Daytona 500.

We stayed on the pole until Jeff Gordon came out to make his run. He turned a blistering lap and bumped us to the outside of the front row. Still not a bad place to start, especially for a rookie.

All of a sudden, life changed in a big way. While the media had been attentive and good to us prior to that run, the interest in our team and us multiplied 20 times or more. The attitude toward our team changed slightly in the garage. All of a sudden, we went from being just one of the great crop of rookies to the limelight and the object of everyone's curiosity. It went from slightly overwhelming to almost unmanageable in 46.249 seconds.

I was determined not to let the short-term success of our qualifying interfere with the next step in our plan, to race well in the 125, learn the draft, and learn how the car would handle in traffic.

Mike Skinner, Ernie Irvan, Jeff Burton, and, of course, Bobby Labonte offered advice and encouragement as to how to handle the outside pressures at the same time as doing the job.

Despite finishing a disappointing 28th after an engine problem derailed his first-ever Daytona 500 effort, Stewart found that his super speedway experience proved to be valuable. *Kristin Block*

Here, he puts that experience to good use at Charlotte, North Carolina. *Harold Hinson*

We raced fairly well in the 125, and I got a lesson from some of the veterans on how the draft works and what happens when you don't have a partner—part of the initiation into Winston Cup by the veterans. It's almost like a rookie orientation class—lessons you can't learn in a book.

To say I wasn't nervous on race day would not be truthful. I just put my mindset in it-is-just-another-race mode and kept focused on the newest task at hand—running 500 miles at Daytona.

Once they said, "Gentlemen, start your engines," it was time to go to work, and everything else faded into the background. Again, I got rookie lessons in drafting from the veterans, but I kept my cool and tried not to make mistakes that would cost us by crashing the car. Then came the engine problems for Bobby and me, and the hopes of a solid finish for me and a win for Bobby went out the window with the wind.

I was, amazingly, not as disappointed as one would think, because so many more positive things happened during my first Winston Cup Speedweeks; I truly felt like we had accomplished all of our goals.

It is also amazing how quickly you put it all behind you and go into next-race mode. Daytona is over, and we are off to Rockingham, North Carolina. But now I am at least a veteran of one thing—I am a veteran of the Daytona 500 and Speedweeks—that is a pretty big accomplishment for our team to be proud of. We did it.

After the ups and downs of his rookie year, Stewart was ready to take on another season in Cup racing.
Nigel Kinrade

Recapping Stewart's First Cup Season

1999 Raybestos ROY Rises in Winston Cup

STAFF REPORT
CIRCLE TRACK, FEBRUARY 2000

It's been a year since Tony Stewart joined the ranks of Winston Cup, and since his first race, the 28-year-old marvel has proven that the switch from open-wheel to stock car racing can be made through hard work, patience, and a positive attitude. The 1999 Raybestos Rookie of the Year has followed his dream by making the transition from the USAC racing to the NASCAR Busch Grand National Series, and now Winston Cup.

That dream began at age eight, when the Columbus, Indiana, native launched his career

The highlight of Stewart's 1999 NASCAR Winston Cup rookie season came at Richmond (Virginia) International Raceway when he scored his first-ever series win. Here, Stewart celebrates his triumph in victory lane. *Harold Hinson*

in go karts. "I grew up interested in racing—my father [Nelson] was a race fan, and he introduced me to racing," Stewart said. "Obviously my heart and the first part of my career belong to Indiana and open-wheel racing at Indianapolis Motor Speedway."

At age 12, he had garnered his first national title in the IKF Dirt Grand Nationals in Oskaloosa, Iowa. By age 19, Stewart had taken eight track championships. From karts, Stewart went to three-quarter midgets, then Silver Crowns—still taking plenty of wins along the way. Eventually, he would make USAC history in 1995 by winning national titles in its three top divisions—midget, sprint car, and Silver Crown—all in one year.

But while he was at the top of the open-wheel game, Stewart had always been interested in joining the likes of NASCAR. "I paid as much attention to the stock car ranks as I did the open-wheel ranks, so I've been aware of NASCAR ever since I was a child," he said.

Stewart's "Triple Crown" win in 1995 led to an offer by Harry Ranier, a former car owner for Cale Yarborough and Davey Allison, to drive part time in the NASCAR Busch Grand National Series in 1996. "Unfortunately, we weren't able to secure sponsorship to keep the team going," Stewart said. Also in 1996, Stewart signed a contract with Team Menard to race in the IRL. He emerged victorious when he won the 1997 IRL championship.

While Stewart was busy in the IRL, Winston Cup team owner Joe Gibbs noticed something special in him and wouldn't let him slip away. "He basically pursued me at all hours of the day and night until we finally came to terms on an agreement early in 1997," Stewart said. He signed with Gibbs to drive the No. 44 Shell Pontiac in the Busch Series in the hope of advancing to Winston Cup.

Crew chief Greg Zipadelli and Stewart quickly bonded to give their Joe Gibbs Racing NASCAR entry the right kind of chemistry. *Sam Sharpe*

Perhaps Stewart could've pushed to enter Winston Cup right away, but he wasn't in a hurry; he wanted to learn as much as he could about stock cars, especially since he had never driven one. "I wanted to get experience," he said. "A race car is a race car in terms of the fact that there are some characteristics that you can apply—but very few in all reality, because open-wheel cars are considerably lighter and have much more horsepower per poundage than stock cars. So, I felt it was better for me to start in the Busch Grand Nationals and learn as much as I could about the stock cars before I moved to Winston Cup."

He gained a wealth of experience early on—of the five races he ran in late 1997, he secured two top 10s and one top 5 finish.

In 1998, Stewart defended his IRL national title while continuing to run in the Busch Series. After competing in 22 Busch races, the team finished off with one second-place finish, two third-place finishes, and one pole.

Now that he had a taste of stock car racing in Busch, it was time to make a choice—whether to stay in the series or move up to the Winston Cup ranks. "He [Gibbs] was not going to push me into Winston Cup if I didn't feel like I was ready," Stewart said.

He wouldn't choose his path alone, however. "When it became apparent to stay competitive in Winston Cup racing, we needed to think about a second team," Gibbs said. The team thought seriously about whether it needed—or wanted—the addition and how it would be assembled. It the end, the group chose Stewart as the driver of the No. 20 Home Depot Pontiac for the 1999 season.

While the organization now has a second car, it is important to note that aside from race days, the crew works as one, not two teams. "We are one team at Joe Gibbs Racing," said Gibbs. "On race weekends, we split into the No. 20 team and the No. 18 team. At the shop, everyone works on both cars. I feel this is the best way for the guys to all work toward the one common goal of having two winning teams."

Stewart's preparedness for the increased number of laps and variety of tracks in Winston Cup stemmed from running in the Busch Series. The lap times he gained on those tracks were an added advantage. "At least it gave me some experience on the tracks that most of the people in NASCAR have been racing on for years," he said. "I had seen most of them—not all of them—but it was helpful. That was the biggest thing I gained out of it."

Although running on a variety of tracks in Busch benefited Stewart, his debut Winston Cup race at Daytona (the Daytona 500) was a challenge. The 2.5-mile track, coupled with the huge crowds at the major Cup event of the year, was a bit startling for Stewart. "It was a little overwhelming because I didn't quite know what to expect," he said. "I also didn't know how the rest of the competitors would view me, but they accepted me really well, so that was not quite as nerve-wracking as I thought it would be." Stewart finished 28th in the February 1999 race.

The Win

Throughout his 1999 rookie season in Winston Cup, Stewart made great strides with at least 10 top 5s, 18 top 10s, 2 poles, and 1 win, at Richmond International Raceway in Richmond, Virginia, in the Exide NASCAR Select Batteries 400. Not only was the win his first in the series, but he also made NASCAR history as the first rookie to win in Winston Cup since 1987, when Davey Allison won at Talladega and Dover.

"About the best way I can describe winning at Richmond: When you take your 10 best Christmases and put them all in one day. I don't know how else to describe it," Stewart said. "It was awesome; it was such a feeling of satisfaction for my team, for Greg [Zipadelli, crew chief] and the guys. It's just the most incredible thing—it's something I will never, ever forget."

Stewart made the most of his 1999 NASCAR Winston Cup debut, winning the division's Raybestos Rookie of the Year Award. Stewart set a record for wins by a rookie in the division with three, besting the old mark of two set by Davey Allison in 1987. He also finished fourth in the division's championship points chase, also a record for a rookie driver in the series.

Other races that stand out in Stewart's rookie season include the Coca-Cola 600 at Charlotte and the Indianapolis 500, both of which he ran on the same day, becoming the second driver since John Andretti to run such a marathon. Stewart, who polished off more than 1,000 miles that Sunday in May, finished ninth at Indianapolis and fourth at Charlotte. Exhausted from not eating enough throughout the day (only a couple of minibagels and PowerBars), he decided to run only at Charlotte and not at the Brickyard next year. Even so, he doesn't regret the chance he had to run the Indianapolis 500.

"I've always wanted to win the Indianapolis 500. It's been a dream of mine. I'd come home from school in May to listen to the radio and find out who was fast and what was going on," Stewart said. "When I made the decision, I was eight years old, and I wanted to be a race car driver. My goal has always been to win the Indianapolis 500, and I'm just grateful for the Home Depot, Joe Gibbs Racing, and everybody who supported that effort to let me have the opportunity to do it [run the race]."

When looking ahead to the next big race, the February 2000 Daytona 500, Stewart plans on treating it like last year's: one race at a time. "Fortunately, we don't have a lot of changes coming to

Above, below, and right
Few drivers have come to the big leagues of NASCAR with the varied background of Tony Stewart, who mastered the USAC Silver Crown ranks before taking the IRL by storm. He then swapped paint in the NASCAR Busch Series before jumping to the Winston Cup ranks in 1999.

the Pontiac, or basically none at all, and we'll just go test down there and get the season kicked off, and try to do as well as or better than we did in 1999."

As Stewart reflects on his racing career, he credits his father, who works for an IRL series sponsor, for helping him get his start in racing—from open-wheel to stock cars. Others who have given Stewart a boost include Larry Martz, the first car owner he drove for in his USAC early years in three-quarter midgets and midgets, and Glen Niebel, the car owner for Stewart's Silver Crown and sprint cars.

Qualities

Of the many factors that play into a driver's success in Winston Cup, attitude is key. To Stewart, who many say has a positive attitude both on and off the track, good self-esteem is vital to staying upbeat. "It doesn't matter whether you're a race car driver or a schoolteacher or a banker or whatever. Attitude makes everything you do," he said. "It makes it easier for others around you to believe in you if you believe in yourself. I just have always tried to keep a really positive attitude about it, about life, and to learn that there are ups and downs and good and bad, and try to roll with the flow."

Patience is another quality that can make or break a driver—especially during the longer Winston Cup races. That was the most important lesson Stewart learned throughout his rookie season. "They're all long races, and you're not going to win them on the first lap. Just take care of the car, the equipment, and the crew, and they'll be there at the end."

As part of a two-car team [with Bobby Labonte in the No. 18 Interstate Batteries Pontiac], Stewart said he realizes that he is probably the weakest link in the team. "I'm the true, true rookie. Everyone else has got at least some experience in Winston Cup. Most of the crew guys have some level, have been on another team, whatever."

At the same time, his teammate has been extremely helpful and supportive, "like a big brother," and that has played into the success of the Joe Gibbs Racing Team. "I'm really lucky to have Bobby Labonte as a teammate," Stewart said.

To Labonte, the addition of Stewart to the team has been a plus for all involved. "His input has been beneficial to both teams, and we share as much information as we can to help us both with our cars," he said. "It has turned out to be a pretty neat deal."

Stewart also feels fortunate to have Greg Zipadelli as his crew chief. Zipadelli, also a rookie, had only a year of experience in Winston Cup before signing on with the Joe Gibbs Racing Team in October 1998. Stewart values the good communication the two have been able to foster, so it's obvious he doesn't want his crew chief to get away. "If I could marry him and my fiancée [Krista Dwyer], I would do it," he said.

On Stewart's progression through Winston Cup, Zipadelli couldn't be prouder. "Tony is probably one of the most talented drivers I have ever seen. He is smart, focused, and dedicated to our race team. When we got to Daytona for the first test last January, we barely knew each other, but it was never an obstacle for us. We went to work learning to communicate from the first day," he said. "We are friends off the track as well."

Stewart had to learn about new cars, new tracks, and new competitors during his 1999 Winston Cup rookie season. Here, one of the all-time great short-track racers, Rusty Wallace (2), schools Stewart on the art of running the Bristol, Tennessee, high banks in a stock car. *Worth Canoy*

Fans and Family

Off the track, Stewart is an avid fisherman, with a preference for bass. He'll fish for anything, anywhere, though. With his full schedule—and a new bass boat—he and the crew try to arrive a half-day or a day early so they can squeeze in some time at the lake. When the weather doesn't call for fishing, however, Stewart can be found playing any sort of NASCAR-style video game, one of his favorites being *NASCAR '99*.

Family is important to Stewart. So important, in fact, that his mother and sister both work for him at True Speed Enterprises, where they are in charge of his merchandising program and fan club. "I depend on them and their contributions to everything immensely," he said.

Fans, of course, are a major part of NASCAR. From those who lounge on their sofas on Sunday afternoons to those who take their seats in the stands, fans have been a crucial part of making the sport what it is today. Stewart has a genuine commitment to his fans, and their support means a lot to him. It's part of the culture of NASCAR and adds to the excitement of racing in Winston Cup. "If those fans didn't fill the grandstands or watch at home on television, there would be no racing or corporations to be in the sport," he said. "It's exciting to see them all in the stands, waving and cheering—whether it's for me or any other driver—with all of their T-shirts and hats."

Just as Stewart has given his time to meet his hometown fans, they took the time to give back to him last May. In Columbus, the city he calls home, are two signs listing his racing accolades. He was also presented with the key to the city. To have enthusiasts recognize him in such a way was heartwarming, to say the least. "I'm extremely honored," he said. "I grew up there. Obviously my heart will always be in Indiana. It was very inspiring, particularly because it's my whole family, and a lot of my friends got to be with me on that day, so that made it real special."

The Future

For Stewart, the future includes not only the chance at more checkered flags, but also wedding bells for him and his fiancée, Krista. The couple, who travel together throughout the Winston Cup season, has set a May 2000 wedding date in Indianapolis. They have been together for about four years, and Stewart recognizes and appreciates the sacrifice Krista has made for him—leaving her home, her family, and her friends—to accompany him from IRL through Winston Cup. "It means a lot to me that she's there. She's been there through the good times and the bad times. We just made a real solid partnership, a real strong friendship, in addition to the romance and then getting married," he said. "She's my lifeline to sanity."

While Stewart is planning to settle down into married life soon, don't count on a career change. Team owner Gibbs looks forward to even greater things this season. "It would be a dream come true to have both Tony and Bobby running for the Winston Cup championship in 2000."

Stewart won't argue with that—he plans to stick around for many more laps.

Three wins, two pole positions, and a fourth-place finish in the final championship standings all pointed to a stellar NASCAR Winston Cup rookie season for Stewart. Here, he points to his pole-winning speed at Bristol, Tennessee. *Worth Canoy*

Roots

Sometimes, Stewart will try to pass in places where there's just no room as evidenced by this wheel-hiking inside move in a UMRA three-quarter midget race in 1997. *Chris Petersen*

Tony Stewart has never given up his ties to or his love of open-wheel racing. It's a part of him, just like being from Indiana.

Stewart still participates in a number of USAC midget races annually, although those numbers have dwindled in recent years. He will also occasionally strap on a sprint or Silver Crown car and has been known to grab the wheel of a dirt late model, basically an open-wheel car with a lightweight body.

When Stewart first made the move to NASCAR, he found the pressures of big-time stock car racing to be oppressive. The off-track requirements of sponsors and fans were smothering. Even the on-track chores of testing and race weekends left little time to relax.

While he admits to enjoying pool, fishing, and bowling as hobbies, Stewart says his real hobby has always been racing. NASCAR made it a job, so it made complete sense that when Stewart wanted to escape the pressures of his job early in his NASCAR career, he went back to what he loved best.

In this case, it meant dominating the 1998 Copper World Classic in Phoenix. Dominating another world—the Indianapolis 500—would prove to be more difficult for Stewart.

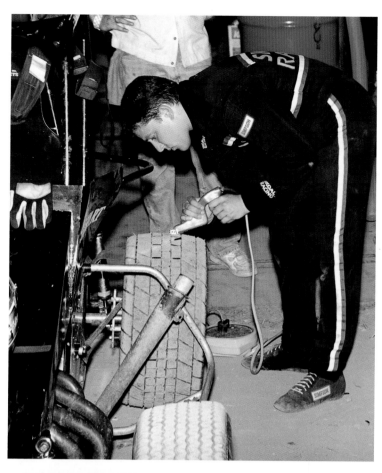

Stewart enjoyed working on his own race cars at the beginning of his career. Here, he uses a tire tool to give his mount a little more bite for the main event. *Chris Petersen*

Stewart has had more than his share of front row starts, including this one with Kenny Irwin (7) in a midget race. *Jeff Taylor*

Stewart's love for dirt racing goes back to his early days as a driver. Here, he (3) hooks up in a three-way battle with Steve Butler (10) and Jack Hewitt (21) in the 1992 Eldora (Ohio) Silver Crown Nationals. *Bob Fairman*

Stewart is happiest when he is sitting behind the wheel of a race car, or in this case, on a race car. *Mark Robertson*

Playing in the Sand

Tony Stewart Toyed with Everyone at the Copper World Classic

STAFF REPORT
OPEN WHEEL, MAY 1998

For Tony Stewart, the Copper World Classic was a chance to play Ferris Bueller. Like the fictional movie character, he took a day off, slipping out the back door to play hooky. Away from the pressure of an IRL title and the business end of stock cars, Stewart went out to play in this big sandbox in the Arizona desert. For the rest of the field, it was like going up against Tiger Woods on a pitch-and-putt.

Stewart's joy at being back in short-track racing was undeniable. When he claimed the midget feature, he pounded the steering wheel with excitement. "When I was poking my fist as hard as I was, I knew I was enjoying it," he said through a wide grin, "and that's what it's all about."

Two races later, he had also won the Silver Crown feature, and he'd come within a tire blister of claiming the supermodified feature as well. Two firsts and a second made him the biggest one-day winner in the Copper World's 21-year history.

Clean sweep. Slam dunk. Runaway. In your face. Whatever the analogy, the result was clear. The competition was scoured clean by a dust storm. Not much left but bleached bones.

Stewart was on the gas in the Copper World Super Modified feature after winning both the USAC midget and Silver Crown portions of the event. *Jim Haines*

Stewart dominated the midget portion of the Copper World action, winning the pole in front of his two Steve Lewis teammates—defending USAC national midget champion Jason Leffler and Dave Steele. Stewart drove away to a three-quarter lap lead in cruising to the easy win. *Bill Taylor*

As the only racer to win the USAC's three short-track championships in the same year, Stewart already wears the crown of "Mr. Versatility." And with an Indy car championship behind him and a full NASCAR Busch Series schedule ahead of him, he certainly had nothing to prove. He had only one reason to be in Phoenix. "Plain and simple, I enjoy it," Stewart said. "Other people play golf for a hobby, but I just get [upset] when I play golf. I'd just as soon climb in a race car."

Not that he took the Copper World lightly. Or the competition, which included six drivers with Indy 500 experience—Kenny Irwin, the most recent open-wheel talent to move on to Winston Cup stock cars, and 16 former Phoenix winners totaling 33 victories among them. This was not a major league pitcher dropping down to AAA for a tune-up. "I take this as seriously as I do driving my Indy car," Stewart said, "but these cars are fun. I'm not running for points. I'm just here to win a race . . . and to see fans that I don't get to see as often as I used to."

In short, Stewart was like any other guy taking a day off. "This is just a release from the business of the other stuff I drive," he said.

When it comes to racing, Tony Stewart is all business. He'd begun his Copper World preparation with a test session in California a few days after Christmas, a session that he shared with supermodified veteran and IRL colleague Paul Durant. Having never driven an offset super before, Stewart stood on the sidelines and watched for a few laps. He then jumped into a strange car, ran a dozen laps of practice—and matched Durant's times. "He was always very professional," said a crew member. "And he seems to have so much confidence that he can do whatever he wants in a race car."

At Phoenix, however, Stewart showed that the key to his versatility is not in willing cars to do his bidding. Instead, like a jockey going from one thoroughbred to another, he has the ability to react to a given car's personality. "I actually drove three different lines with three different cars, especially in turns one and two," he said, referring to the part of Phoenix International that is most critical to fast laps there. "It really depended on what the car wanted to do . . . it was just a matter of learning each one."

Stewart was also quick to credit the cars' respective crews. "As much as I was jumping from car to car," he said, "it was easy to adapt, especially when each one was working so well."

Midgets

The first evidence of Stewart's adaptability came in the midget portion of the program. That Stewart defended his Copper World title from the pole was not as remarkable as the overall qualifying performance of owner Steve Lewis's three-car team. Stewart found teammates Jason Leffler, the defending USAC national champion, and David Steele alongside and behind him. All three cars— each carrying a driver with a distinctly different style—qualified within a tenth of a second. It was a testament to chassis tuner Bob East, who built three identical cars but tweaked each one, a wheel here and a spring there, to tailor-fit the drivers.

Despite a series of red and yellow flags that repeatedly bunched up the field, Stewart cruised in this one, opening up as much as a quarter-lap lead. He also left a traffic jam that included Leffler, Steele, Irwin, and Danny Drinan—in an experimental R&D chassis of his own—to fight over the runner-up spot. Bad luck struck most of the group. Irwin faded, Drinan lost his second engine of the weekend, and Leffler lost the runner-up spot after an extended caution period, during which his engine overheated and prevented the butterflies in the injectors from fully closing, in effect creating a stuck throttle.

The luckiest guy in the midget field was Indiana driver Ryan Newman, who started tenth and finished third, behind Steele. Along the way, Newman definitely finished first on style points. Midway through the feature, he slammed the front stretch wall, did a full 360-degree spin like a turnstile while the field scrambled past, landed wheels down and pointed in the right direction, and continued in the race after losing only one spot. As USAC officials called him into the pits for a safety inspection, he received a large ovation from the grandstands, which got even louder as he was cleared to rejoin the field.

Silver Crown

Again Stewart won from the front row—of the consolation race. After running some of the fastest practice laps of the weekend and the third fastest qualifying run, Stewart found himself shuffled to the consi because of the USAC rulebook. Pit lane traffic for the Silver Crown cars was thicker than Manhattan at rush hour. "Every time the Silver Crown cars went out, there were 60 of them in line while some guys were trying to get into their pit box," Stewart complained. He burned out his clutch trying to hold the car in the stop-and-go jam on pit lane. The George Snider–led crew sweated and strained to replace the clutch, but missed the car's turn in the qualifying line by more than three spots, automatically making him ineligible to qualify outright for the feature.

Terror with four wheels. That's the best way to describe Stewart's Copper World Super Modified entry. *Jim Haines*

In winning the consi, Stewart turned laps even faster than his qualifying time, but still fretted over starting 25th in the feature. "We're going to need some luck and yellow flags," he contended. "We'll automatically be five seconds behind the leader when the green flag drops."

It wouldn't have mattered if he started five days behind. "You never count yourself out, and 50 laps is a long race for a big car," Stewart said.

He needed only half that many laps to rocket through the entire field. His margin of victory, about 10 car lengths, included a cushion of five lapped cars.

Stewart credited crew chief George Snider "for keeping me pumped up on the radio" during his march through the field. The win was also a vindication for the Silver Crown veteran and co-owner

A. J. Foyt. "I've been a bridesmaid here five times in supers and champ cars, so this feels really good," Snider said.

The win was extra-sweet for Stewart, too. "I believed I could win this from the get-go," he said, "but I didn't want to win this one like I did Las Vegas." This was a reference to Stewart's first-ever Silver Crown win last year, in which on-track contact eliminated Donnie Beechler from the title chase. "Today," he said, "I feel like I've really won a Silver Crown race."

Supermodifieds

For the third year in a row, California driver Troy Regier found himself starting on the front row and worrying about tires. He was convinced that his rubber wouldn't last for more than a half-dozen laps. In the end, the tires held up just long enough to prevent Stewart from claiming a hat trick.

Although the grid included 24 starters, this was a two-car shoot-out from the drop of the green flag. Even supermod veteran and IRL driver Davey Hamilton, who has won this race four times, couldn't get any closer than 20 car lengths to Regier and Stewart.

Unhappy over excessive tire wear, Regier made wholesale changes to the car overnight in an all-or-nothing gamble. "I ran only eight laps in practice before we ran out of tire, so we had to do something," he said. "We changed the roll center height, tire stagger, wing angles . . . everything."

Stewart's crew also gambled on a chassis change, and it cost them the race. After Stewart led the opening laps, the race was stopped to give cleanup crews a chance to clear the racetrack after a multicar tangle. "These cars hate to be loose," said car owner Larry Triguero, "so during the red flag we loaded more weight in the left rear and made the car too tight."

Stewart was already running about an inch less tire stagger than the other front-runners, and the chassis change made the handling that much worse. Later, Regier said he was able to pass for the lead because Stewart was too loose and drifting high in the turns. But what Regier probably saw was Stewart trying to shake and manhandle the car so it would turn.

For Regier, who finished second in the supers' season-long West Coast points battle last year, the win was a step forward from last year's runner-up spot in the Copper World. And it topped a day in which he was also the only rookie to qualify for the Silver Crown feature. "It hasn't sunk in yet," he said as he draped the victory wreath around his neck. "I'm just a farm boy from central California. I'm just going to get on my tractor Monday and relax."

Tony Stewart's win in the 1998 USAC midget portion of the Copper World Classic at Phoenix, Arizona, looked vaguely familiar. He poses in victory lane after winning the same race a year earlier in the 1997 edition of the Copper World Classic. *Steve Koletar*

Forgiveness

"I just wish we could have done the job for him in the supers," a crew member said wistfully about Stewart's near hat trick.

Stewart himself was grateful for his history-making day. "Anytime you can win a race it feels good, and when you win two it's even better," he said. "Anybody would trade me for that today."

Stewart's tally for the Copper World matched his performance in the 1995 Four Crown event at Eldora, where he won the midget and sprint features and took the runner-up spot in the Silver Crown main. "Eldora is my favorite dirt track and Phoenix is my favorite pavement track," Stewart said, "and now I've come up with the same results in both places."

Stewart acknowledged that his continuing career in short-track machines is causing heartburn for his NASCAR owner, Joe Gibbs, who would prefer that Stewart focus more on his upcoming Busch Series schedule. "But what are you gonna do?" Stewart said with a shrug. "This is the kind of racing that got me where I am."

Nonetheless, he acknowledged that "this may be my last play day for quite a while."

As he prepared to leave Phoenix for an IROC test session in Daytona, he still had to answer to Gibbs. "He didn't know about the supermodified," Stewart coyly confessed. "I thought it would be better to ask for forgiveness than permission."

Not a bad thing to ask the rest of the field at Phoenix, either.

# of Pure Desire

STAFF REPORT
OPEN WHEEL, SEPTEMBER 1998

Stewart has never been a very good loser, but the biggest winners seldom are. So what?

For three years he has lit up the Indianapolis Motor Speedway, lit it up like few newcomers ever have. Never mind that Tony Stewart has not yet managed to win the 500; every May since his rookie run there in 1996, he has been the best story—"Dirt Track Kid Makes Good"—going into the race. It is the postrace story that has been a problem.

In 1996 he was a rocket all month, starting from the pole and leading convincingly until his engine quit, leaving him 24th in the finishing order. Last year he qualified in the middle of the front row, dominated the first half of the race, struggled in the second, and tried so hard to make something happen in the closing laps that he bounced off the fourth-turn wall on his way to fifth place. This time around he came out of the second row, took the lead with a dramatic traffic move on lap 21, and then lost the race with equal drama just one lap later with another engine failure. He finished dead last.

Three 500s, no wins. Plenty of fireworks, though. Lord, has he ever been something to watch at 16th and Georgetown.

If you want to list all the drivers who went from bullrings to the Brickyard and stood the joint on its ear as quickly as Stewart has, you jot down the names Bill Vukovich, Parnelli Jones, and Jim Hurtubise, and then you put away your pencil. Thus far, of course, he has more in common with

While Stewart's passion has been to win the Indianapolis 500, the race has never been that kind to him. Here, he is on the hook back to the garage area after a mechanical breakdown just one lap after taking the lead. *Allan Horcher*

Hurtubise, the speed demon who never conquered the Speedway, than with Vuky or Jones, each of whom won the 500 on his third try. But he has plenty of Parnelli in him, too, and plenty of Vukovich: the Saturday-night roots, the meteoric climb, the notion of Indianapolis as the end of some personal rainbow.

Here was Stewart on ABC television, in the hours before this year's 500: "I'd give up every win and every championship I've ever earned in my life to win this race just one time. I'd give up everything I've done in the 27 years I've been alive."

That is saying something because Stewart has done a few things: two USAC national midget titles, one each in USAC's sprint and Silver Crown divisions, the 1997 IRL championship. And yet I believe what Stewart said; I believe he would trade it all, straight up, for a chance to have his face carved on the Borg-Warner trophy.

In that same TV interview, he spoke of his "pure desire" for Indianapolis. It is a passion that manifests itself in the way he has driven the place, right from day one back in 1996. Look at the number of practice days over the last three Mays, all of which have ended with Stewart and Team Menard setting fast time during Happy Hour; look at the all-out qualifying efforts every year; look at the way he stalked Greg Ray into traffic in this 82nd running of the great race, and then shot by

Stewart won the pole and turned the fastest lap of the race in the 1996 Indy 500, only to have an engine failure derail his run to victory lane. *Ken Coles*

him with maybe the most authoritarian pass for the lead since Rick Mears went around Michael Andretti to steal the victory in 1991.

And look at the way it ripped Stewart's guts out when his car smoked to a halt on the very next lap. His pit road interview, again on ABC-TV, told you everything you needed to know about Tony Stewart and the Indy 500.

Team Menard put a fast car under Stewart for the 1996 and 1997 Indy 500s, but Stewart came up short of victory. Here, the team works on the car at Charlotte, North Carolina, during practice for a 1997 IRL event. *Harold Hinson*

"This is the only thing I've ever wanted to do in my life," he said. "This has been my number one goal."

He paused. "And every year, I get shit on doing it."

Then he stalked back to the Menard garage and spent the rest of the afternoon refusing to so much as acknowledge the pack of reporters who waited outside to hear from him. For this he was beaten up in the papers for the better part of a week, which just goes to show that the racing press has gotten so used to being spoon-fed generic quotes from losing drivers—"I had a great race car, we were right where we needed to be until we broke, and God bless my sponsors"—that it has forgotten how to deal with honest emotion.

The whole thing brought to mind a great passage by writer Ross R. Olney, who had this to say about Bill Vukovich's fury at dropping out while leading the 1952 Indy 500: "Vukovich was blistering mad. Gracious in defeat? He was a terror. He brooded, then ranted and raved, then brooded some more."

Forty-six years later, it has apparently become too much of a bother to paint such imaginative word pictures. And so we get Robin Miller, the *Indianapolis Star* columnist, suggesting that Stewart "grow up" or perhaps "get Huggies as a sponsor."

Tony Stewart's eyes tell the story as he unbuckles after a less-than-desired run during practice for the Indy 500.

Look, Tony Stewart was a terrific story at Indy, even in defeat. He was a terrific story, even with his mouth shut. He is 27, still raw, and he is not much on hiding his feelings; if you watched him walk back to Gasoline Alley, his head down and his face an angry crimson, you didn't need a sound-bite to know what was on his mind. Stewart himself seemed to understand that better than some of the attending journalists did.

A few days after the 500, he said of the reporters camped outside his garage, "I knew they were going to ask me two things: 'What happened?' Well, they could have gotten that from [team manager] Larry Curry and [team owner] John Menard. And, 'How do you feel?' I mean, how did they think I felt?"

He had a point. He had been forced out of the biggest race of his life—because Indianapolis is exactly that, every year—in the middle of another passionate performance. Didn't his silence say enough? Or have we gotten to the point where we expect our Indianapolis heroes to drive like Jim Hurtubise and act like Miss Manners?

Here is the bottom line: Tony Stewart has never been a very good loser, but the biggest winners seldom are. So what?

When you drive with pure desire, sometimes racing breaks your heart. Vukovich could not smile with a broken heart in 1952, and Stewart could not do it in 1998. It is the same story. Maybe we just knew how to write it better back then.

The Drive to Win Fuels a Temper

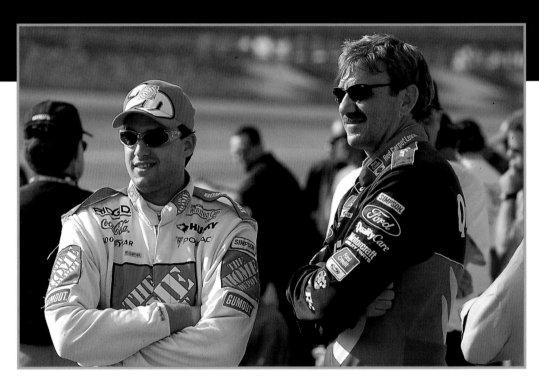

Like Stewart, Dale Jarrett has had his share of gripes about on-track incidents, fans, and NASCAR over the years.
Paul Melhado

Here's a quick quiz:

Name the term that best describes Tony Stewart:
A. Tony the Terrific
B. Tony the Terrible
C. Tantrum Tony
D. Taciturn Tony
E. Tony the Tremendous

In reality, all of them have been correct at one point of Tony Stewart's tumultuous racing career. Stewart's mood swings both in and out of a race car are legendary and have drawn the notice of fans and the ire of the media since he burst on the national scene in the mid-1990s.

One minute quiet, reserved, and humble, the next shoving his way through the media and fan hordes, Stewart has fashioned an image that at times has put him in damage control mode. In that regard, Stewart is not unlike the rest of us as he tries to make his way through life.

An angry Stewart is collared by a NASCAR official as he storms pit road after a race accident. At times Stewart has shown that he has trouble controlling his temper. This has made him the object of scorn with fans and media alike. *Rusty Husband*

In his case, however, Stewart's life is laid bare in front of the world to see. If he has a transgression of any kind, on or off the track, it's either going to be televised live to the world or in the national press the next day. It's a daunting challenge knowing your every move is going to be scrutinized, but that's the reality of being a public figure in today's media- and entertainment-driven society.

Stewart is not the first, and he won't be the last, to be taken to task by the media for his actions on and off the track. A. J. Foyt had epic battles with the media. Dale Earnhardt had a comfort level with reporters, but he never truly cozied up to the working press. Neither did Bill Elliott. Others, such as Darrell Waltrip, Jeff Gordon, and new stars such as Jimmie Johnson and Jamie McMurray, have used the media to advance their careers.

In the following chapters, Stewart's behavioral transgressions are examined along with his relationships with the media, fans, NASCAR, and his competitors. Never one to pull a punch, Stewart has to duck some here.

Strap on the gloves and headgear—it's time to get it on.

Joe Gibbs Racing teammates Tony Stewart and Bobby Labonte are driven on the track and almost opposites off it when it comes to temperament. Stewart can be volatile, while Labonte is laid back and relaxed. *Paul Melhado*

Tony Stewart is able to put all the distractions and pressures of racing aside when he straps in for a race. According to most drivers, it's the only real place they feel "safe." *Paul Melhado*

Tony's World

By Ron Lemasters Jr.
Open Wheel, June 2000

Tony Stewart is sitting on top of the world these days, or at least close enough to the top not to have to worry about what the view will be like when he gets there. He's young, he's rich, he drives a hot car with lots of power, and he has access to all the power tools he could ever use. In addition, he has the respect, admiration, and loyalty of many racing fans from coast to coast and everywhere in between.

So why isn't he happy? Most of us would sell our souls—or even our Saturday night Knoxville Nationals tickets—for a chance to have anything close to what he has.

Stewart is at his happiest when he is driving winning race cars. Here, Stewart is obviously enjoying himself as he holds the winning trophy in victory lane at Richmond International Raceway after capturing his first Winston Cup win in 1999. *Kristin Block*

Of course, selling our souls to the Prince of Darkness might just allow us to be as talented behind the wheel as the young Mr. Stewart, but it's a pretty good bet we wouldn't. Talent such as Stewart possesses at such a young age comes from the opposite direction.

That leads us back to the question: Why does it seem Stewart is not enjoying himself these days? To be quite honest, it seems like the young man is positively, unequivocally miserable with a capital *M*.

He's been seen snapping at fans seeking his autograph. His general disdain for members of the Fourth Estate rivals that of famed pitcher Steve Carlton, who went nearly a full decade without uttering a printable word to the assembled scribes/tape jockeys. And at Daytona, he locked horns with another open-wheel driver whose mercurial nature has sent him on more trips to find himself than any 10 survivors of Woodstock.

Stewart squared off against Robby Gordon, the bad boy of

For the most part, Stewart's temper has not gotten the best of him on the racetrack. That wasn't the case at Bristol Motor Speedway in spring 2001 when he dumped Jeff Gordon on pit road after the race. Here things go more smoothly for Stewart on pit road during a routine stop for fuel and tires at California Speedway. *John Pyle*

open-wheel/desert/stock car racing, following an on-track skirmish during an early-week practice session. Stewart took exception to Gordon's actions and vice versa. A powder keg had been building under the Rushville Rocket, and that's a bad thing when the damper on your mouth isn't always grabbing the slack from above your eyebrows.

Gordon walked down to Stewart's garage for a little consultation, and the rest, as they say, is forever preserved through the magic of videotape. As fisticuffs go, it was more worthy of an amateur club fight in Hoboken than a Vegas title match. Although the two are in the same weight class, more or less, and both entered with unbeaten records, it looked more like a spat between the preppies on *Beverly Hills 90210* than the *Friday Night Fights*. Neither driver landed a punch—unless you call Stewart's dismissive shove to the shoulder of Gordon's driving suit a left hook, and all Gordon did was hold. Well, that's not exactly true. He grabbed the front of Stewart's uniform and held on while the younger driver's eyes popped.

It really was no big thing. There's more fighting in line at the Selinsgrove concession stand during hot laps than Gordon and Stewart provided. The real problem, in my opinion, is why it happened at all.

Why isn't Tony Stewart happy? He might tell you he is, and he sure has reason to be after last year and the start of this one. But there's a feeling here that it's just too much. Too much attention, too many people clamoring for a piece of his time and energy, and too few places he can go to make it work within himself. The only place it all goes away is at the racetrack with his sprint car or midget or IRL car, and he doesn't appreciate being disturbed while recreating, thank you very much.

"I had more fun last night at Volusia Speedway Park with the sprint car than I have had all year," Stewart said while waiting to do an interview for TNN Sports. "I can stand around the hauler and talk and not be bothered all that much, and when it's time to race, we go race. It's not like here," he said, pointing out the window at a garage full of people, some of them

Winning soothes the competitive beast that lives inside Stewart as evidenced by his smile in victory lane after a win at Dover, Delaware. *Nigel Kinrade*

obviously having nothing to do with race teams or racing and others just hanging around.

There's frustration in his voice, and in everything he does, or so it seems from this angle. I honestly think the only thing keeping Stewart from bagging all this and returning to open-wheel racing is the fact that the money's better in stock cars these days and so is the TV deal. Besides, he has a contract with Joe Gibbs Racing that has a few years yet to run.

I guess the point is that Stewart is in a box that he helped build, and it's too late to decide that the box is a little claustrophobic once you're inside. There is a trade-off between what one wants and what one needs, and I think Stewart has somewhat of a burning need to be away from the constant press and fan attention for a while. If Joe Gibbs would let him, I think Stewart—using an assumed name and in disguise—might just run three or four races a week in between stock car events and be happy as a veritable clam. But that'll never happen, given the climate these days. Sponsors, team functions, and photo shoots are more a part of the game than some mundane thing like a driver's feelings or needs.

In case those of you scoring at home even care, I called it a draw, because Stewart led with the left and got inside Gordon's guard, but Gordon recovered well and took no damage.

Fighting, along with many other activities once openly embraced by members of the motorsports set, is no longer part of the curriculum taught at your local track. But sometimes, when it gets right down to the no-bull business of dealing with yourself, there simply isn't any other choice—especially if you're getting fed up with fame and fortune, and the box you live in is controlled by somebody else.

Stewart is happiest when he's on the track, away from the crowds that fill the garage area. *Sam Sharpe*

Temper, Temper

If You Want to Come to the Party, Be Prepared to Dance

By Bob Myers

Circle Track, November 2000

Tony Stewart has won a couple of races since publicly airing his personal frustrations with NASCAR Winston Cup racing. Those wins, no doubt, helped reshape his attitude toward facing the many hassles that accompany the fame his success in this sport has given him. Stewart said he loves racing, but all the other distractions that come with Winston Cup racing are making him miserable. We figure Stewart, last year's rookie sensation, was simply frustrated and feeling the pressure because he hadn't won the first several races this season.

Stewart has been one of the most vocal drivers in NASCAR when it comes to media and fans. At times, he's had to do damage control after offending both groups with his comments. *Paul Melhado*

You needn't be told that Stewart said in a May interview that his life was miserable and he was fed up with NASCAR. He said he was tired of dealing with fans, media, and the hassles of the Winston Cup Series—including overcrowded garage areas, fans who hound him for autographs everywhere he goes, intrusions on his private life, people who try to control what he says, and drivers unwilling or afraid to speak their minds. Naturally, that upset many racing fans, who booed him at the next Winston Cup race (at Lowe's Motor Speedway). Stewart's comments also didn't sit well with his car owner, Joe Gibbs; his primary sponsor, Home Depot; and many of his fellow drivers.

Damage Control

Three weeks later, Stewart did a little damage control. He said he stood by his comments, but they didn't paint the big picture accurately. He said he was frustrated and overwhelmed by the demands on his time that he had not anticipated when he came to Winston Cup last year. He stressed that he loves the fans and that one major reason for his outburst was he didn't have enough time to spend with them. It's OK for fans to be in the garage area, he continued, but there are so many of them, he lets some of them down because he can't satisfy all of them. (Stewart previously had refused to sign any autographs while in the garage area.)

Our perception is that Stewart is an exceptional talent and basically a decent guy—so long as things are going his way. Some would say he's spoiled, perhaps a cut above being bothered. True or not, his most obvious weakness, by his admission, is his inability to rein in his temper. Stewart's honesty, emotion, and outspokenness are refreshing in a sport that has become somewhat antiseptic. We wouldn't want that to change. But there is a point at which refreshing becomes rude.

Over the years, one of Stewart's biggest gripes has been about the overcrowding in the garage area. NASCAR allows select fans, sponsor representatives, and media types into each event. On the track, however, crowds are not allowed.

Stewart has spent much of his brief but remarkable Winston Cup career making apologies and doing damage control. That's OK, but at some point he must get control of his temper, or his situation will worsen as his star continues to rise. Winston Cup racing is a tough sport—on and off the track. But attitude and temperament shouldn't be dictated by whether you win or lose. The idea that Stewart can be a regular guy, as he'd like to be, is merely an illusion.

Rookie Pressures

Granted, Stewart was thrust into a unique situation last year. As the first Winston Cup rookie driver to win three races and finish as high as fourth in the championship standings, he became an instant star. No rookie had ever faced the attention, demands, and commitments Stewart did for at least two reasons: The magnitude of his accomplishments were unmatched among rookies, and Winston Cup has more fans and is getting more attention than ever before.

Still, it is difficult for us to grasp that Stewart, an IRL champion, came into the Winston Cup Series blind to the circus-like atmosphere that surrounds its stars. In fact, none of the hassles seemed to get under his skin until this year—when he didn't win in the first dozen races. When he did win at Dover, fans cheered him, and that was sweet music to his ears, he says. He should know that fans will also cheer and support him when he doesn't win—if they like him.

It is hard to have sympathy for Stewart, given his success and the millions of dollars he's earning. Unless we're myopic, the way we see it is if anybody in Winston Cup is happy, it should be Tony Stewart. He's not by any means the only driver to lose his privacy and be confronted daily with the demands and obligations of stardom. At what price glory? And consider those in Stewart's midst who have not tasted stardom and would relish putting up with practically anything to swap places with him.

Hindsight is 20/20, but if Stewart had taken his dilemma to Gibbs first, there wouldn't have been a public outcry or controversy, and he could have saved himself a lot of grief. Gibbs, a former Super Bowl champion coach of the Washington Redskins, knows all about fame and how to deal with it. Moreover, he's a gentleman of the highest caliber.

We've always been impressed with Jeff Gordon's behavior off the track. Gordon didn't win a race his rookie season, but we all know what he's done since. With uncommon humility, youthful awe, and few complaints and criticisms, Gordon handled his transition from a NASCAR nobody to the sport's biggest star like the champion he is. That's in spite of fans booing him every race because he whipped the butts of the establishment all too often. There might be a lesson here for Stewart.

He Does Have a Point

We do understand where Stewart is coming from, however. Winston Cup garage areas, once a haven for drivers and crews, are overcrowded. It's a growing pain. NASCAR has the unenviable task of controlling the garage area. For each event, NASCAR issues garage passes to speedways to cover media, staff, teams and their sponsors, and NASCAR sponsors, said Kevin Triplett, NASCAR's director of operations. So how do the unaffiliated, the autograph seekers, and picture takers gain access to the restricted area? Well, you know, through friends, connections, favors . . .

Drivers will tell you they don't object to fans in the garage, but they readily admit that there are too many allowed in. It's a tough conundrum: sign all the autographs and not spend enough time doing your real job, or concentrate on your job and risk offending your fans? Of course, if you spend too much time with your fans and your performance on the track suffers, you're going to lose the fans anyway.

Perhaps NASCAR needs to treat these growing pains. Triplett said the sanctioning body has discussed establishing designated times when drivers will be available to fans in the garage. "We've talked about two or three scenarios, and when we find one we think will work, we'll do it," Triplett said. Maybe there should be a no-autograph policy in the garage, no detaining of drivers

Early in his career, Stewart didn't seem to mind the attention as evidenced in this 1996 shot from a Legends car race at the Pepsi Coliseum at Indianapolis. The crush of media surrounding NASCAR, however, has been problematic for Stewart at times. *Jack Gladback*

Stewart's personality has its upside. He gives his time willingly to many charitable projects, including Habitat for Humanity. *Nigel Kinrade*

for photographs except by the working media. What about controlled and timed autograph sessions with drivers at their souvenir trailers? That's also difficult. Any time a driver leaves the sanctuary of the garage area, there's the chance of starting a "feeding frenzy."

The issue here is not overcrowded garages. It's the broader issue of the accessibility of drivers and participants, a premise on which Winston Cup was founded. It is a relationship unique to pro sports, a tradition and an expectation that is not going to change.

But gone are the days when drivers like Richard Petty, who set the standard for fan interaction, sat for hours signing autographs until everybody who wanted one got one. Sheer numbers render that standard unapproachable. It is sad, Petty said, but true. At the track, drivers are prisoners of their motorhomes and haulers, or so it seems.

Stewart's Peers Weigh In

Few drivers speak out about their plight because they don't want to embarrass their car owners, sponsors, and themselves—not because they're fakes.

"I think it will be tougher on him [Stewart] because of what he said," Mark Martin said. "That's why you don't get those type of comments from other drivers because they know

nothing can be gained. I share his pain, but I don't have an answer. Racing is very popular because part of its foundation is accessibility, and Tony Stewart or myself isn't going to change that."

"We have to be very careful what we complain about," added Jeff Burton, who is extremely busy and has his act together as well as anybody, "and we have to be careful how we complain about it." Burton doesn't want to be a star, either. "You can make it as hard or as easy on yourself as you want it to be," he said. "I choose to live my life as if nobody knows who I am. I go to dinner. I take my daughter to the zoo and to dance class. You can choose to let it worry you, or you can choose to ignore it. I choose to be responsible in what we are doing and do the right thing."

"I don't care who you are," said two-time Daytona 500 champion Sterling Marlin, "you can get too big for your britches, and it can cost you. Not a single one of us is bigger than the sport."

When you have a determined driver like Tony Stewart, you need an equally understanding owner. Stewart has that in Joe Gibbs who, along with crew chief Greg Zipadelli (left), tries to keep Stewart balanced both competitively and personally. *Harold Hinson*

Even after winning the Cup championship in 2002, Stewart still had a love-hate relationship with the media. *Nigel Kinrade*

Above
Wins in Cup come with a price, one that Stewart has been reluctant to fully pay. *Sam Sharpe*

Right
Stewart's on-track ability is unrivaled by most Cup racers. He is working on his off-track behavior, though. *Harold Hinson*

"Plain and simple, this sport isn't bigger than the fans," said John Andretti. "They made us what we are. We have a legacy to continue. It's not always what you say—it's the way you act that people remember."

"I've given every ounce of myself to racing for 25 years, and I will continue to do that until I'm finished," concluded Martin.

It's quite evident that for most drivers, the opportunity to race and achieve stardom at the Winston Cup level is worth the sacrifice. Apparently, though, the sacrifice is not for everyone.

Tony Tirades

BY BENNY PHILLIPS
STOCK CAR RACING, MARCH 2003

If you let him, Tony Stewart will turn you against stock car racing, free of charge. He is to the coming Winston Cup season what Bigfoot is to a camping trip. You never know when he will embarrass you as well as himself.

Usually, when he makes one of these pinheaded moves it leaves a giant track through the sport. Then he wants you to forgive him, and keep on forgiving him, and most of all, he wants you to believe him.

But his promises go unfounded in sincere warmth, and his broken promises stand out like a pig in a peanut field. Some of the most unruly of NBA players are better heroes.

There was a time when NASCAR stood proudly, and fans even bragged that "our sport" runs without the disruption experienced in major league sports. Drivers went out of their way to get along with the media. They understood the media helps fill the grandstands. These guys were always available.

Richard Petty made a habit of staying in one spot, usually pit wall or the back of his truck, and signing autographs until dark or later for long lines of fans. He was the kind of champion who fans and media alike hoped would reign forever over the sport. He was not the only one who showed kindness to fans and media.

All was tolerable with champions that followed. Darrell Waltrip would get on his chopping block occasionally, and sometimes Dale Earnhardt could be as sullen as an old country judge sitting on a cactus spur.

The stress of a hard day at the "office" is evident on the face of Stewart as he straps in for another NASCAR Winston Cup race. Facing the battle of competition and the responsibilities that come with being a top driver in the series has been tough on him at times. *Nigel Kinrade*

Stewart had an especially hard day at the 2003 Daytona event, when he finished last in the standings.
Nigel Kinrade

Bobby Allison would express his opinion—good or bad—about what you were doing. But it was all in the family, a happy family that fans loved and the media respected.

Then along comes this mad publicity raven who, because of NASCAR's negligence in allowing a driver on probation to continue running over media members in the garage area, ends up as Winston Cup champion.

It could only happen in racing. Even a sanctioning body for goat roping would have suspended Stewart on the eve of the final race of the 2002 season, but apparently probation means little in NASCAR anymore.

Let's take a look. At Daytona, after the July 2001 race, Stewart slapped a tape recorder from a reporter's hands, then kicked it under a truck. NASCAR placed its problem driver on probation for the rest of the year.

At Indianapolis 2002, Stewart got out of his car and in the garage area punched a photographer. He drew a fine by NASCAR and received a $50,000 fine from his major sponsor.

Stewart promised the world he would do better. He enrolled in an anger management program. He is a changed person, he said. Within a few days a lady files a complaint in Bristol, Tennessee, claiming Stewart shoved her after the race there. A Tennessee grand jury debated an assault case against Stewart, but the case never went to court.

Stewart doesn't want to be bothered again here at the 2004 Daytona 500.

Following the race at Rockingham, Stewart used a word that TV partly censored when describing his car. NASCAR often fines competitors for using vulgar language, but the sanctioning body overlooked it this time.

Then on the eve of the season's finale, Stewart hammered another photographer in the garage area at Homestead, Florida. Photos from the scene clearly show that Stewart had an acre or so to get by the guy.

NASCAR lets it ride. Remember? Stewart promised the world he would do better. The temper management class is helping, right?

The truth is that it's impossible to believe anything Stewart says, particularly about his future. He has brought this upon himself. He could be a fine example for the sport, for kids, for fans, for media. But a role model he is not.

It would be absolutely wonderful if our Winston Cup champion makes it through this season without making a spectacle of himself. I for one hope he does, and I believe many of you feel the same way.

He will never be a Richard Petty; it's not in him. But a year from now it could be a story of success, of how the champion changed his acrimonious ways and became a role model.

But if Stewart goes through another year like 2002, then it's time to write him off as "Bam Bam" Tony and pass him on to another circuit.

The many faces of Tony Stewart, from his days in the midget ranks through the IRL, NASCAR Busch, and Cup Series. Like most professional athletes, Stewart might waiver off the track at times with the fans and the media, but there can be no doubt where his focus is once he is strapped into a race car.

James Compton

Rick Nelson

Ron McQueeney

Steve Cessar

Dennis Krumnocker

Nigel Kinrade

Success in Winston Cup

While Tony Stewart has proven he can be successful in almost any kind of race vehicle, it is at NASCAR's highest level where he has made his greatest mark.

From his first laps at Daytona International Speedway in February 1999 you knew Stewart was going to be something special. Blazing speed and a front-row starting berth in NASCAR's biggest event are bound to draw some attention.

Throughout his inaugural Winston Cup season, Stewart continued to impress, notching his first career NASCAR win at Richmond and following it up with two others to set a Winston Cup record for wins by a rookie, breaking the mark set by the great Davey Allison. A fourth-place finish in the championship standings, also a Winston Cup rookie record, was Stewart's at the end of the season.

In 2000, Stewart doubled his win total from the previous season scoring six victories, but fell to a "disappointing" sixth in the final championship chase. Three more victories, and a second-place finish in the points followed in 2001. If there were any questions that Stewart was destined to become one of NASCAR's greatest modern-era drivers, he answered them in 2002 by backing up his USAC and IRL titles with three wins and his first NASCAR Winston Cup championship.

Stewart's three Winston Cup wins in his 1999 rookie season bested the old mark of two victories by a first-year driver. The prior mark was set by Davey Allison in 1988. *Kristin Block*

Clearly, Stewart is gifted when it comes to sitting behind the wheel of a NASCAR stock car, or any other race car for that matter.

As documented, achievement and fame are crowns that haven't always set well upon the head of Tony Stewart. In the following chapters, Stewart addresses fame, fortune, notoriety, and NASCAR as only he can and dares to do. We look at why Stewart, or any other driver, has trouble defending a title in the modern world that is NASCAR racing.

Joe Gibbs' decision to bring Stewart to the NASCAR Winston Cup ranks in 1999 paid off when Stewart started winning races. *David Garrett*

The *Stock Car* Interview

Tony Stewart

By Jason Mitchell
Stock Car Racing, November 2002

*It's like freedom
of speech doesn't
exist when it
comes to
NASCAR.*
—Tony Stewart

At times in your career, you've been labeled as one of the sport's bad boys mainly because you say what's on your mind. Then again, some of the greatest drivers in NASCAR history, such as Darrell Waltrip and Dale Earnhardt, have done the same thing. Do you feel like that adversity fires you up?

I didn't realize speaking my mind made me a bad boy. That's what kind of confuses me about that labeling. Just because I speak my mind makes me a bad guy? I thought that's what our country was all about. It's kind of odd because people should be honest. I guess it's getting more and more like wrestling every day because people don't really take things for what they are anymore. When I go to a short-track race and watch those drivers, I see fans who are respectful of their time and let them do their thing. After the race is over, they can come down and talk to the driver and get autographs. It's kind of a weird era now because our sport is turning into the WWE [World Wrestling Entertainment] to a certain degree. I guess if speaking your mind makes you a

Nigel Kinrade

127

Being competitive and beating people on the racetrack is what Stewart is all about. Here, he celebrates a Winston Cup victory at Richmond (Virginia) International Raceway. *Harold Hinson*

bad boy then there are millions of bad boys in this country. There are so many penalties and negatives that go along with speaking your mind in this series, that's why you don't see that with a lot of the other drivers. It's like freedom of speech doesn't really exist when it comes to NASCAR.

During driver introductions before the start of a race you are, hands down, one of the three or four guys that get the biggest response, whether the fans are cheering or jeering. Does hearing people boo when your name is called bother you, or do you believe that as long as they're making some kind of noise, that means you're getting the job done behind the wheel?

That's exactly right. There are 42 other drivers who start each race and, like you say, we're one of three or four guys that 100 percent of the people, whether they like or dislike you, will make some type of noise for. It seems like now I'm about 50-50 as far as the fans go. I don't think hearing the fans booing me is such a bad thing anymore.

You made the comment a couple of years ago when talking about some of your past mistakes that there was no guideline of how a Winston Cup driver was supposed to think and act. As you've matured, what have you learned from that aspect of things?

I don't know if it's maturing so much as just seeing the handwriting on the wall. That goes against everything your parents taught you growing up as a child. When you get in my position, you learn that honesty is not the best policy. Even if you're right, some people don't want to hear it. They've got a picture of how they think things are, and that's the way they want it to be.

If there is one thing that you've done in Winston Cup racing that you could take back, what would that be and why?

It would be a lot of the things I have said as well as some of the actions I've done. It has really taken away from what I was trying to do in the car. With our sport as clean as it is, anytime you do anything just a little bit off par, it really gets blown out of proportion. If anything, I would have learned in 1999 to roll with the punches and do like most of the other drivers in giving out vanilla answers instead of waiting until 2002.

If there were one thing or trait in yourself that you could change, what would that be?

I guess I would want to be more passive. There are a lot of things that I don't agree with, and I know they aren't right, but I'm not in a position to change them. The people who are in a position to change those things don't really care to change them right now. If anything, I suppose I would want to be able to close my eyes and ears and let things just go on by because I can't change them. Most people don't get to see some of the real problems in our series; but at the same time, if you start talking about those things, you start seeing problems from other directions.

Before the season started, you made the comment that you were going to eliminate outside distractions, such as dealing with the press, in order to focus on the task at hand. Has the media been easier to work with this year?

I don't think so. Dealing with the media for 38 weekends a year allows you to learn a lot about the individual reporters. You learn which ones you can trust and which ones will stab you in the back in a heartbeat. It wasn't that we wanted to eliminate a lot of the media. We just wanted to be very selective about who I did interviews with. We've had to prioritize whom I give that time to. If it's a reporter I've had problems with in the past, they've proven they're not worth my taking the time to do interviews with them. We keep a list of who are the friends and who are the foes, so I am very selective about the members of the media I will spend time with.

What's the best thing NASCAR has going in its favor and one area the sanctioning body could improve upon?

The best thing is the people. The fans of NASCAR are the best group of fans in the world. You can't find more passionate and dedicated fans. As far as what I think could be done to make it better, people need to realize that this isn't wrestling. As much as it's about the show, the reason NASCAR got as big as it has is because they put on good races. It's not about the politics and NASCAR making all this money they're making these days. Race fans shouldn't have to pay the prices they're paying now to go see a Winston Cup race. Right now, it's just a little bit ridiculous.

After finishing last in the season-opener at Daytona, you've had an uphill battle as far as the points race was concerned. What was the key to getting back into contention for the championship?

We didn't do anything different than what we normally do. It's just because of the fact that we as a team have all been able to do our jobs. Even after Daytona, we got off to a much better start than we normally do. Once we reached that point early in the season, it was just a matter of trying to be consistent.

You've said that, for whatever reason, you've been a slow starter as far as the points race is concerned. What has been the difference this season? Are there any certain areas you can pinpoint?

Not really. We tested at Las Vegas and that helped us a great deal when we raced there. I think a lot of stuff we learned at that early test, as well as some things we found last fall, really helped us to get off to a good start this year.

Many have said that with your past in open-wheel racing, you would never feel as if your career was complete without winning the Indianapolis 500. Do you really feel that way?

I think I've had a good career no matter what happens in the future. If my career ended tomorrow, I would feel like it was a great one. Sentimentally, I really do want to win the Indianapolis 500. Then again, I don't know if I'll ever do that race again after last year. It's hard to say what I'm going to do because it is so hard trying to do both races. It's getting harder and harder to try and run that race when I'm not running in that series on a regular basis. I feel like some of those guys are getting ahead of me as far as the technology and setups. For me, it's just hard to try and focus on running the Indianapolis 500 because I'm trying to win the Winston Cup championship.

How much help do you think your open-wheel racing background translated into success in stock cars?

I think a race car is a race car because they all have four wheels, a brake, and a gas pedal. So I don't think it's that big a difference between open-wheel and stock cars. With my running the midgets and the sprints, I probably learned to drive a loose car a long time ago.

What advice would you give to young drivers with aspirations of making it to Winston Cup racing?

I'd tell them to make sure this is what they want to do before they get here. With million dollar contracts and multiyear deals, once you are here you're here until all those contracts are done. From the outside looking in it looks great, but it's a lot of hard work. Young drivers need to make sure this is truly what they want to do. I love the sport and people involved in Winston Cup racing. All the officials and people in this sport are great to be around, but to me some of the politics takes away from how good it could really be.

A rough travel schedule and demands on his time are anything but a dream life according to Stewart. When it comes to driving a race car, however, Stewart lives the dream millions of fans can only fantasize about. *Nigel Kinrade*

Stewart is one of the top three or four drivers when it comes to drawing a fan response during driver introductions. While the fans who boo used to bother Stewart, he says they don't anymore. *Sam Sharpe*

How much do you miss the good old days of Friday and Saturday night racing?

I miss them every single day.

As far as your racing career goes, what motivates you the most?

Winning is what it's all about. To be able to go out on the track and beat people and be competitive, that's what it's all about. There's not a better feeling in the world.

You're a young, single driver, living what almost anyone would consider a dream life. How far from reality is that when you take into account the time you're away from home?

Anybody who thinks I'm living a dream life, they're the ones who are dreaming. I have not been home in two and a half weeks to do stuff I've wanted to do. Being able to go out and run some of the short-track races I've done recently has been fun. In all reality, there have been a lot of things I love and enjoy that I've not had the time to do. There is a price. For every amount of success and fame you have, you lose part of your personal life along with it. Right now is a perfect example, because while I'm talking with you, my girlfriend and buddy are at the mall shopping. I'd much rather be hanging out with her, but you know as well as I do there is no way I could spend two normal hours at the mall. That's just unrealistic. It doesn't mean the people are bad; they just see you and they get all excited and it starts drawing attention to where you end up doing an autograph session at the mall. It's not a big glamorous life, but when I was racing in the Busch Series I thought it would be. Once I got in this position, I realized I couldn't do all the normal things I was used to doing.

Stewart says he wishes he had "rolled with the punches" instead of speaking his mind at times. Still, the driver continues to be one of the most controversial when it comes to commenting on NASCAR and some of its policies. *Harold Hinson*

At this point in your life, have you started to think about getting married and having children, or are you still just concentrating on your racing career?

I'm probably still more focused on my racing career than anything. I've met a really neat girl from California who I've been seeing and I enjoy spending time with her. She's a little bit younger than me and isn't in a hurry either. So we're just kind of enjoying each other right now and not in a big hurry to do anything.

If you had a job outside of racing, what career path do you think you would have followed?

I've never really thought about it because I've always been involved in racing in one form or another. There was one year that Dad and I ran out of money and I had to quit my go kart racing. I ended up being the assistant flagman at the track instead.

What active driver in Winston Cup racing do you admire the most?

There are a lot of guys who I really look up to. One of those drivers is Ricky Rudd. I admire him because of his honesty. I admire Mark Martin because of how smart he is during the races. I also admire my teammate, Bobby Labonte, for taking the amount of time that he has taken to spend with me as well as all his work to get me where I am in my career. So there are a lot of drivers I look up to for each of the aspects they bring to the sport.

When fans think of the name Tony Stewart, what do you want them to think of?

I want them to think of me as someone who was competitive at everything he ever drove. I've won championships in midgets, sprints, and Silver Crown cars all the way down to go karts. That's how I want people to remember me. Knowing I was competitive and won races in every type of car I've ever driven is probably the thing I'm most proud of right now.

What do you think you'll you be doing 25 years from now?

I'll be racing, but it won't be in Winston Cup. There are a lot of things in Winston Cup racing that are going to have to change before it will become tolerable again. I see things getting a lot worse before they get better in our sport. In my conversations with some of the higher powers, it looks like there are a few of us who see the handwriting on the wall and it's hard to believe that they don't. There will be a time when I say I've had enough and I'll be ready to move on. Until then, I'm going to continue to give 110 percent.

What is the perfect day away from the track for you?

Being able to go to a midget or a sprint car race and not having to answer any questions about Winston Cup racing. That's perfect to me.

A driver is only as good as his pit crew and Stewart's Joe Gibbs Racing is one of the best. Clockwise from above, the No. 20 cracks off position-gaining stops at Pocono, Daytona, Dover, and Charlotte. *Christopher Pasatieri, Nigel Kinrade*

Winning Is the Best Medicine

By Bob Myers

Circle Track, April 2003

Winning and celebrating his first NASCAR Winston Cup championship might prove to be better therapy for Tony Stewart than anger-management counseling.

Stewart may have a new perspective on the magnitude and meaning of winning the championship of the world's premier auto racing series, not measured by $4.3 million in bonuses and the obligatory praise heaped upon him and the No. 20 Home Depot/Joe Gibbs Racing team. Maybe Stewart understands now why he was pestered by the media with questions about the title chase six weeks before the fact. In 23 years of racing, Stewart, 31, had won an assortment of eight championships, including the open-wheel Indy Racing League's, but none is comparable to this.

Perhaps learning that he has earned the support and respect of his fellow drivers and others around him and the experiences associated with the ultimate achievement in his profession will change Stewart's sometimes ugly attitude and suppress his hot temper. He has promised, with his right hand raised, that will happen.

A bad-boy public image, which we believe tarnished Stewart's title and probably cost him national driver of the year honors, can't be erased overnight, but this is a new year that starts with a clean page. While Stewart richly deserves the spoils of his accomplishments on the track, his kid-like, temper-driven episodes of misbehavior are in the back of the minds of even those who paid tribute to him. He is the only driver to

Stewart fought through his share of distractions on and off the track to stay focused and win the 2002 NASCAR Winston Cup title.
Jon Riles

Winning can often take the sting out of bad days at the racetrack. Stewart has won his share of NASCAR races, including this victory at Dover International Speedway in 2000. A Winston Cup title and nearly $20 million in earnings in 2002 can also salve plenty of wounds.
Sam Sharpe

Stewart has been able to make light of his bad boy image by poking fun at himself. In 2002, Stewart made and wore a T-shirt with the slogan "Obnoxious Talladega Race Driver" on the front. The move got plenty of laughs and plenty of press. *Harold Hinson*

win the Winston Cup crown while on probation. He embarrassed himself, his team (which he almost wrecked at midseason), his car owner, his sponsor, his fans, and his sport with inappropriate conduct and poor judgment, mostly run-ins with NASCAR and the press.

Stewart is not a bad guy. His intense passion for driving race cars and winning races is a virtue until it fosters a lack of discipline and self-control when things don't go his way. He abhors losing. He is easily irritated and frustrated by certain off-track obligations and expectations most top drivers readily perform with civility, like it or not.

Stewart doesn't have to be a cookie cutter or a conformist. He can be outspoken and rebellious, admirable and refreshing traits to a point, and different if he chooses. But continued defiance of NASCAR and the media, and he will suffer unnecessary grief and ridicule.

The Tony Stewart millions of us saw in person or on television during the NASCAR Winston Cup championship activities and awards ceremonies in New York was delightful, personable, and charming with a keen sense of humor. He was, in his words, "a regular media darling" for a week.

He tried to make up with NASCAR and the press. He promised to do a better job dealing with the media. He appeased others he has offended or disappointed with lavish praise. Was he sincere? Time will tell.

On a visit to a New York police precinct during his demanding, whirlwind New York tour, Stewart said, "Police officers . . . get such a bad rap without people really knowing them as a person. I can relate to them because if you spend a half hour with me, I'm not that bad a person." That's true. As Winston Cup has mushroomed and flourished, drivers are spread way too thin. They have

From the looks on the faces of crew chief Greg Zipadelli and Stewart in this victory lane shot from Phoenix, Arizona, there's no stress in Stewart's winning ways right now. *Drew Hierwarter*

become protectively inaccessible. The garage area at most tracks is not a sanctuary but a zoo, a condition that has festered for several years and remains unchecked by NASCAR. Unlike the old days, there is precious little opportunity for media or fans to really get to know drivers and crews personally. Unfortunately, impressions are made from a distance, based on what is seen and heard.

No doubt Stewart has formed lasting impressions of his own during his early months as champion, none that impacted him more than one of the first after the championship became reality at Homestead. He described his slow drive down pit road with members of rival teams lined up in tribute to him as "priceless." He was particularly moved by the presence of crew chief Ben Leslie and runner-up Mark Martin's team, who had battled him for weeks and lost. "No matter how big the check Winston writes, how many trophies I win . . . my peers taking time to congratulate me is probably what I am going to remember and respect most about this championship," Stewart said.

So Close

Martin was the sentimental favorite to win his first championship. His fourth second place and 12th finish among the top 6 during the 15 years that he has driven for Jack Roush makes us wonder why the powers that govern stock car racing continue to tease and deny a deserving man of his talent, record, and character. That's our sentiment for old-timers Sterling Marlin and Ricky Rudd, too. The quintessential Winston Cup driver, Martin has earned the respect and admiration of his competitors, including Stewart's. Is there time for Martin, who turned 44 on January 9, to know the

Despite his Cup championship, Tony Stewart is still struggling to learn how to deal with disappointment on the track. *Nigel Kinrade*

joy of a championship? Stewart is convinced there is. "Don't ever doubt you will be [champion], because you will," Stewart said to Martin.

It would have been touching and fitting had Martin or one of Jack Roush's teams given the popular car owner his first Winston Cup crown to replace his trademark floppy brown or straw hat for a night. Maybe Roush used up all the miracles when he survived the crash of the small plane he was piloting and was rescued from an Alabama pond by ex-Marine Larry Hicks.

But the fact that Roush Racing's teams dominated the season shy of the title in a complete reversal of 2001 was consoling balm. The four Ford teams won 10 races, logged 40 top 5, and 75 top 10 finishes and were second, third, eighth, and twelfth in the points standings. No one else was close. "Nobody has been able to make that many cars run that good," complimented Joe Gibbs, who has a handful of championship rings, two Winston Cups, and, as coach of the Washington Redskins, won three Super Bowls.

Martin, with a win at Charlotte in the Viagra Ford and a series-low 12.2 average finish, rebounded from a winless 2001 and from 12th to second in points. Matt Kenseth led the circuit with five wins and sold lots of DeWalt tools. Dynamic young Kurt Busch put the bounce in Rubbermaid with four wins, three of the last five, sealing third in points. Jeff Burton, Roush's sole Winston Cup winner in 2001, fell below his standard sans a win, but all of the teams finished strong enough to be considered title contenders this season.

Looking back, Tony Stewart's championship was a remarkable feat under dire circumstances in a strange season of uncommon excellence by youthful drivers and bittersweet performances by leading multicar outfits. Stewart and his irrepressible crew chief, Greg Zipadelli, who single-handedly kept the team focused and motivated in spite of distractions and turmoil, are to be warmly congratulated.

At the same time, Stewart ought to be ashamed. For four years he's been a spoiled problem child, precisely the right word. He's 31, time to grow up. He is an immense driving talent and huge star, with 15 wins, fourth, sixth, second, and first in points, and $20 million in earnings. But he doesn't know how to lose, can't grasp that he can't win them all. In 1967, Richard Petty won 27 races, which would be near perfection in this era, but he lost 21. Loosen up, Tony. Be happy and grateful for where you are and what you've done. Send the babysitter home. It's a pity the media has to dilute an otherwise glorious and momentous career milestone by writing about this stuff. Enough is enough.

One at a Time

Stewart's Failure to Repeat as Champ Is a NASCAR Trend

By Larry Cothren
Stock Car Racing, November 2003

Listen to Greg Zipadelli, crew chief for Tony Stewart, and you quickly gain insight into why Stewart won't successfully defend his Winston Cup title this season. A notoriously slow starter, the Home Depot team came out of the blocks stronger than ever this season, Zipadelli points out, and even stood second in points after the race at Darlington in March. Then the season turned sour.

Stewart finished 25th or worse in six of the seven races following Darlington, including consecutive finishes of 41st, 41st, and 40th.

First, there was a disaster at Bristol in a race that began the team's troubles. "Even after getting a fender torn off and bending a ball joint we were still going to salvage what had been a bad day, which is what you do when you're in the championship hunt," said Zipadelli. "Then an oil line, because of one of the wrecks, got pinched and killed the motor. We end up 30th."

The hard luck continued. "Then it was Texas [and a 34th]," continued Zipadelli, "running eighth or ninth, and we lost a motor with 30 to go."

The predictable struck at Talladega, where Stewart finished 25th. "We were in a wreck and we had had a very strong car," added Zipadelli.

Martinsville's sixth-place finish was the lone bright spot, before California was the scene of an engine failure—and a finish of 41st. Richmond brought a crash and another 41st. At Charlotte, engine failure produced a finish of 40th.

Zipadelli lists his team's misfortunes in the first half of the season with the scripted nonchalance of a corporate CEO standing before a board of directors and defending his company's sudden drop in the stock market.

But there's no script for the bad racing luck that has plagued the No. 20 Home Depot team this season. And this is not a crew chief making excuses

Stewart posed for his hero card "beauty shots" prior to the 2003 NASCAR season. It would be a less than satisfying year for the defending division champion. *Brian Czobat*

Greg Zipadelli managed Stewart to the 2003 NASCAR Winston Cup championship, but a string of mechanical problems and bad luck midway through the 2003 campaign sidelined a run for two titles in a row. *Harold Hinson*

for rotten performance. This is one of the top wrenches in the sport offering analysis on his team's woes. Zipadelli's delivery is as unscripted as one of the five engine failures his team experienced in the first half of this season.

Yet Zipadelli understands that trying to explain bad racing luck is as hopeless as making up 717 points—the margin Stewart faced from 11th to first after 23 races—in the final third of the season.

"Now why is all this happening?" he said. "Did we lose all of our racing luck toward the end of last year because we had a lot of good fortune and had things go our way? It sure isn't because of lack of effort or performance from our cars or especially our driver.

"It's probably more frustrating for me on the inside, not being able to give you an answer for our problems, than it is for someone like yourself trying to come up with something to explain to people on the outside."

The conclusion—if there is indeed a conclusive explanation—is that a championship performance demands near perfection, particularly with the parity that marks NASCAR's top division.

The run by driver Matt Kenseth and crew chief Robbie Reiser provides the current example, and most assuredly there'll be another next season. Kenseth, with just one win in the season's first 22 races, has had few crippling performances in 2003. Just when it appears disaster is ready to strike, Kenseth and Reiser pull off another strong finish. Zipadelli can relate. He and Stewart worked their way from dead last in points, following the 2002 Daytona 500, to the title, giving team owner Joe Gibbs another championship to go with the one earned by Bobby Labonte in 2000.

Stewart spent plenty of time in the garage area in 2003 (here at Richmond) and eventually finished seventh in the final NASCAR Winston Cup championship standings with 2 wins, 12 top-5, and 18 top-10 finishes.
Harold Hinson

Now Kenseth and Reiser are poised to give team owner Jack Roush his first Winston Cup title—barring disaster, something that appears unlikely.

"They can't do anything wrong," observed Zipadelli, turning his crew chief's analytic eye from his team to another. "They've had stuff happen to them and it turns around and the caution falls right in their lap. I'm not talking bad or begrudging them, but I'm jealous as hell. You know what I mean? They're running well every week; they're doing what they've got to do; and they're doing a great job."

This Is the Season

In a perfect world, this would be Tony Stewart's championship year. From the disastrous start at Daytona in February 2002, to Stewart's well-documented off-track troubles, the intense, sometimes volatile driver endured more adversity last season than many drivers experience in a full career. Home Depot's unprecedented $50,000 fine against Stewart, after Stewart allegedly struck a photographer, was the low point. There were also reports of troubles between Stewart and Zipadelli and Stewart and his other Home Depot teammates. Given Stewart's problems, the team's ability to win the championship last year was, above all else, a testament to resiliency.

There appears to be a new Tony Stewart this season, however. His flare-ups are at least of the low-profile variety. He told the Associated Press' Mike Harris earlier this year that he "got tired of being angry." To deal with his volatile temperament, Stewart brought in a sports psychologist midway through the 2002 season. He says he's learned to relax, maintain his cool, and not let the myriad of distractions in the sport get under his skin.

Considering the team's problems this season—situations that most often have been out of Stewart's control—the new mindset couldn't have come at a better time. Stewart sounds like a motivational speaker when analyzing his team's midseason problems, far different from the angry man he became during trying times last season.

"It's been just little things here and little things there," Stewart said. "It's not been anything huge. I think all you guys [the media] expected me to flip out this year with the way things have gone, but we're running good. We're doing everything right. We just haven't had the luck to go with it. Having last year over with and out of the way and the stress of that being gone, it's helped put things in perspective. If we were running 25th to 30th or something, and blowing motors and having something happen, it would be harder to deal with.

"[Zipadelli is] putting great setups on the cars. The guys are building good cars, good bodies, good motors. All the ingredients have been there to win races all year, [but] it's a matter of having everything go our way. When you have a year like we had last year, we needed a lot of luck at the end of the year to help get us up to where we were. That's what happened: We had good luck. My grandfather's turning out to be a genius. He said everything makes a full circle, and it has. It went from everything being really good at the end of the year to things starting off to kind of going south for us.

"Now, hopefully, it's coming back the other side of that circle and we're finishing that cycle. There's nothing you can do about it. I think I've probably dealt with it better than Zippy has this year. I'm the one inside the trailer at the end of the day trying to find the positives in every negative this year. It's kept us with an open frame of mind to say, 'Hey we're doing everything we need to do; it's just a matter of getting luck on our side.' With that in mind, it has let us stay focused for the next week and not dwell on the past week."

While the sports psychologist no doubt helped the man dubbed "Tony the Tiger" deal with the stress of a Winston Cup campaign, there's nothing quite like a Winston Cup championship to ease an angry mind and soothe the psychological wounds of failure.

"It just seemed like once we won the championship last year, it was like a weight was lifted off our shoulders—like I dumped a 3,000-pound weight off my back," Stewart said. "As a race team, this year we've had more fun. Between the guys on the crew and myself, we've really enjoyed our racing this year. That's something we'd started to lose in the past.

"As much as we all loved the sport, we were losing the passion behind why we love it so much. We needed to get that back, and luckily winning the championship did that for us."

As an NFL coach for several years and as a Winston Cup team owner, Gibbs has dealt with every temperament and situation imaginable in sports—and he's provided a steady, guiding hand for Stewart in good times and bad—but Gibbs has noticed a dramatic change in his driver. "We've had a lot of things happen to the car this year and he doesn't seem to get nearly as uptight and rattled by it," Gibbs said. "He's much more relaxed."

No Repeat Title

Stewart's inability to repeat as champion is part of a pattern in the sport. He's the fourth consecutive champion who has failed to repeat. Since Jeff Gordon's back-to-back championships in 1997 and 1998, the last four champions—Dale Jarrett, Labonte, Gordon, and Stewart—have faced the same dilemma. That points to the parity in the sport, which is fueled by the most intensively competitive period in Winston Cup history.

It's tougher than ever to win a Winston Cup title, and repeating as champion has become next to impossible. Significantly, three of the last four to win the title were first-time champions.

Stewart scored just two wins in 2003, one of them coming at Pocono (Pennsylvania) International Raceway and the other at Lowes Motor Speedway in Charlotte, North Carolina. At left, he celebrates his Pocono win. *Harold Hinson, Nigel Kinrade*

"When you win the first one, it's so overwhelming and there's a lot to sink in," said Gordon, a four-time champion. "A lot of times you won't see guys win back to back after they've won their first one. I didn't win back to back after my first one. I won back to back after my second one and I think that was because I knew what to expect. I knew how the schedule was going to go. I knew how to say yes to things and how to say no to things.

"When you're a first-time champion, a lot of times you don't say no to anything. You're like, 'Man, I'm Winston Cup champion and I want to do all the things and be the best Winston Cup champion I can be.' Then all of a sudden, you find yourself going, 'Wow, this is a lot of stuff and this is really wearing me down.' "

Stewart downplays the notion that winning the championship has actually taken focus away from this season. In typical fashion, he even places blame on the media for overstating the impact a title has on a champion's personal life.

"I've looked at myself as one of the 43 guys that starts the race every Sunday," Stewart said. "I think [representing the sport as champion] was built up too much to be honest. I'm not going to say it's disappointing, because it's actually been very pleasant for life to go on as usual—contrary to the belief of some of the media members. I've enjoyed it. There has not been anything unpleasant about it by any means. There have not been any added demands like everybody speculated. It's just been business as usual for us."

Zipadelli concedes that there are minor distractions that come with being the championship team, but says the chase itself may be the toughest element in winning a title.

"I think a lot of it is that you work so hard toward the end of the year where you, like we did last year, just try to win the championship, and we weren't working as hard on this year as we could have been," said Zipadelli. "And I don't mean that in a bad way, to say we didn't work, but maybe we weren't focused on it. Like right now [in mid-August], I've already got cars and chassis and stuff

Stewart had more than his share of bad luck in 2003, including a wreck at Richmond International Raceway in the spring. *Harold Hinson*

for next year. That's how far ahead I am this year, where last year I didn't start that stuff until the end of the year because I couldn't. We just didn't have the time or energy to do it."

The key to repeating a title, Gordon said, is to always be thinking ahead to next year. That was part of what made crew chief Ray Evernham and the Hendrick Motorsports organization so successful during Gordon's championship runs in 1995, 1997, and 1998.

"Ray is a very intense, very focused guy, and I can remember going through the '97 season when we were battling for the championship and he was already thinking about the following year," recalled Gordon. "I think through the experience of '95 and '96 [when the team failed to repeat], it kind of put us in a position to really know how to do it differently if you're ever in that position again. I think that is where Ray was really good and he kept that team focus on the future at all times. It was like, 'Yeah, we're going to go out there and win this championship in '97, but we're not going to lose sight of what we've got to do the next year to win it again.'"

Adapting to Change

Zipadelli said the notion that a championship team falls behind because of a reluctance to change and adapt in a rapidly changing sport—essentially standing pat and negating its chances of a repeat title—has been disproven by the Home Depot team. Circumstances dictated that staying the course was not an option for the team in 2003.

Stewart and his team toughed out switching from Pontiac to Chevy in 2003. *Nigel Kinrade*

The Gibbs organization made a switch from Pontiac to Chevrolet this season, bringing with it the need to build new cars—18 Zipadelli said—and placing more emphasis than normal on testing. The team had to develop new packages to adjust to the brand change. The result—outside of the engine failures and other misfortune—has been a team capable of running up front. Despite the early setbacks, Stewart won this season's first Pocono race. He also led 11 of the first 22 races, and his 511 laps led were fourth most on the tour after the Watkins Glen race, while he was the leader in miles led with 915.

"We've been running well," Stewart said soon after the Pocono win. "We've had better cars than we've ever had, better engines, the best bodies we've ever had on our cars. It's just a matter of everything falling into place, finally.

"When you go out and lead the laps that we led at Charlotte, [and] run as hard as we did at Dover, the Winston, California—you look at all those places—and we were doing our job. But we didn't have the luck on our side. We knew in our hearts that it was just a matter of time before it finally turned back around in our favor."

That, no doubt, was spoken by a man very much in touch with his emotions and with his place in life.

Gordon makes a point that may prove prophetic, considering Stewart's willingness to change. "You've got to change with the times if you want to stay successful," Gordon said. "That's one of the things I admired so much about Dale Earnhardt and Richard Petty and guys like Terry Labonte, people who won championships over several years in this sport. These guys were able to adapt to the times and the changing conditions of the cars and the tracks."

While Stewart leads the rest of the pack here, he couldn't repeat his Cup championship run in 2003. *Nigel Kinrade*

It took the No. 20 team and Stewart some time to adapt to the Chevy Monte Carlo before he could find success on the track. *Nigel Kinrade*

Daytona Dreams, 2004

Stewart started 5th at the Daytona 500 in 2004; on this lap he's bearing down on Jeff Gordon. *Nigel Kinrade*

Joe Gibbs Racing came out strong in 2004: Stewart in 2nd and teammate Bobby Labonte finished 11th. *Sam Sharpe*

Daytona 500 winner Dale Earnhardt Jr. gets a congratulary hug from runner-up Stewart. *Harold Hinson*

Based on results alone, Tony Stewart is already a Hall of Fame racer. His accomplishments—an IRL championship, four USAC titles, including three in the same season, a national go kart title as a youth, and his most recent achievement, a NASCAR Winston Cup crown—are the stuff legends are made of.

If Stewart were to retire today, his place as a motorsports icon would be secure. The reality is Stewart, still in his early 30s, is nowhere near retirement. His age, along with his skill and competitive drive, are going to have fans cheering him for years to come. One can only imagine what Stewart's final career statistics will be once he hangs up his helmet for good.

Stewart is already accepted as one of the greatest drivers in the history of American motorsports and is regularly invited to participate in the International Race of Champions event.

Of course, there will be challenges. Many of his NASCAR contemporaries—Jeff Gordon, Matt Kenseth, Jimmie Johnson, and Ryan Newman—are also young and still in the early stages of their careers. Winning at the NASCAR level is only going to become harder as these drivers mature and new, even younger, challengers change the dynamics of the sport.

Stewart will also have to master himself if he is to flourish and survive in today's marketing driven world of racing. More and more a vehicle to sell products rather than a celebration of speed, racing, especially NASCAR, isn't looking for drivers who rock the boat. Only those who agree to pull the oars in the same direction need apply.

A complex, driven man, Stewart may eventually flame out at the NASCAR level because he can't, or won't, conform to the corporate image that is required in today's sponsor- and media-friendly racing model.

Then there's still the specter of the Indianapolis Motor Speedway and the Indy 500. Stewart grew up in the shadows of the famed Indiana racetrack and has had a lifelong, burning passion to win "the Greatest Spectacle in Racing." Will he return to Indy to chase his dreams of winning the 500, or will NASCAR consume his time and perhaps, eventually, his spirit to compete?

Only time will tell.

Until then, enjoy the ride that is Tony Stewart. Just as we originally compared him to a legend of another era—A. J. Foyt—future generations will try to make those same comparisons to Stewart.

It will be a tough act to follow.

Will Stewart ever return to compete in and win the Indianapolis 500? Still in his early 30s, one can only guess what racing worlds Stewart has left to conquer. *Kristin Block*

No matter what Stewart does in the future, he will probably still find a way to make a name for himself. *Nigel Kinrade*

Birthdate:	May 20, 1971 (Columbus, Indiana)
Resides:	Cornelius, North Carolina
Height:	5 feet 9 inches
Weight:	165 pounds
Marital status:	Single
Hobbies:	Boating, fishing, pool, bowling

NASCAR CUP SERIES CAREER SUMMARY

Season	Races	Wins	Top 5	Top 10	Poles	Points	Rank
1999	34	3	12	21	2	4774	4
2000	34	6	12	23	2	4570	6
2001	36	3	15	22	0	4763	2
2002	36	3	15	21	4	4800	1
2003	36	2	12	18	1	4549	7
Totals	176	17	66	105	9		

NASCAR BUSCH SERIES CAREER SUMMARY

Season	Races	Wins	Top 5	Top 10	Poles	Points	Rank
1996	9	0	0	0	0	753	49
1997	5	0	1	2	0	459	57
1998	22	0	5	5	2	2455	21
2003	1	0	0	0	0	140	109
Totals	37	0	6	7	2		

NASCAR CRAFTSMAN TRUCK SERIES CAREER SUMMARY

Season	Races	Wins	Top 5	Top 10	Poles	Points	Rank
1996	1	0	0	1	0	134	94
2002	1	1	1	1	0	180	69
2003	1	1	1	1	0	180	85
Totals	3	2	2	3	0		

IRL CAREER WIN SUMMARY

Date	Race Name	Track	Starting Position
6/29/1997	Pikes Peak 200	Pikes Peak International Raceway	2
1/24/1998	Indy 200	Walt Disney World Speedway	1
6/28/1998	Pennzoil 200	New Hampshire International Speedway	6

IRL CAREER POLE SUMMARY

Date	Race Name	Track
1/25/97	Walt Disney World	Walt Disney World Speedway
3/23/97	Phoenix	Phoenix International Raceway
6/7/97	Texas	Texas Motor Speedway
7/26/97	Charlotte	Charlotte Motor Speedway
1/24/98	Indy 200	Walt Disney World Speedway
6/6/98	Texas	Texas Motor Speedway

USAC CAREER CHAMPIONSHIPS

Silver Crown	(1) 1995
Sprint Car	(1) 1995
National Midget	(2) 1994, 1995

USAC CAREER WIN STATISTICS

Silver Crown	3
Sprint Car	10
National Midget	27

Index

Agajanian, Cary, 36, 37, 50, 64
Agajanian, J. C., 36
Alboreto, Michele, 38, 39, 51
All Pro Bumper to Bumper 300, 53
Allison, Bobby, 58, 121
Allison, Davey, 85, 87, 124, 126
Andretti, John, 118
Andretti, Mario, 57, 58
Andretti, Michael, 60, 103
Barker, Ray, 15
Barker, Roy, 11
Beechler, Donnie, 18, 99
Boat, Billy, 15, 19, 21, 43, 44
Brickyard 400, 16, 79, 87, 101
Bristol Motor Speedway, 53, 70, 90, 91,
   110, 121
Buhl, Robbie, 38, 39, 45, 49, 51
Burton, Jeff, 74, 82, 118, 143
Busch, Kurt, 143
Butler, Steve, 21, 26, 94
Calkins, Buzz, 30–32, 36–39
Carter, Pancho, 21
Championship Auto Racing Teams (CART), 30,
   32, 33, 36, 40, 51, 52, 64
Charlotte Motor Speedway (Lowe's Motor
   Speedway), 83, 87, 104, 143, 144
Cheever, Eddie, 32, 35, 36, 38, 51
Chevrolet, 151
Chili Bowl, 14, 54
Chrisman, Steve, 15, 16
Coca-Cola 600, 63, 87
Copper World Classic, 42, 92, 95–100
Craven, Ricky, 58
Curry, Larry, 39, 45, 49, 56, 61, 104
Darlington Raceway, 67, 144
Daytona 500, 54, 56, 58, 66–68, 81–84, 86,
   117, 121, 136, 145
Daytona International Speedway, 59, 67, 76, 84,
   89, 109, 124, 130, 146
Dismore, Mark, 49, 51, 79
Dover International Speedway, 87, 111, 115,
   152, 136, 138
Drinan, Danny, 18, 19, 97
Earnhardt, Dale Jr., 67
Earnhardt, Dale, 76, 77, 107, 120, 127, 152
East, Bob, 17, 21, 97
Eldora Four Crown Nationals, 16, 17
Eldora Silver Crown Nationals, 21, 94, 100
Evernham, Ray, 58, 151
Exide NASCAR Select Batteries 400, 87
Food City 500, 70
Ford Motor Company, 54, 56, 63, 143
Ford Thunderbird, 56
Formula One, 32, 38, 45, 51
Foyt, A. J., 21, 31, 36, 40, 42–45, 49, 54, 57,
   58, 60, 64, 76, 99
George, Tony, 30, 36, 39, 51, 54, 56, 57, 64, 73
Gibbs, Joe, 55, 59, 62–66, 68, 72, 76, 80, 81,
   85, 86, 91, 100–112, 114, 115, 117, 126,
   143, 145
Goody 250, 53
Gordon, Eric, 16

Gordon, Jeff, 52, 58, 60, 66, 70, 73, 76, 107,
   110, 111, 115, 143, 150, 151, 156
Gordon, Robby, 79, 109
Guerrero, Roberto, 31, 32, 34, 36–39, 43
Hamilton, Davey, 18, 30, 36, 38, 40–45,
   49, 50, 99
Hartman, Butch, 21
Hearn, Richie, 31–33, 36, 37, 51
Helmling, Rollie, 24
Hemelgarn, Ron, 34
Hendrick Motorsports, 151
Hewitt, Jack, 16, 17, 76, 94
Hood, Rick, 21
Hurtubise, Jim, 101, 105
Hut Hundred, 11, 12, 21
I-44 Speedway, 11
IKF Dirt Grand Nationals, 15, 25, 85
Indianapolis 500, 12, 16, 30, 32, 36, 45, 51, 54,
   57, 58, 60, 61, 64, 79, 80, 87, 92, 96,
   102–105, 130, 156
Indianapolis Motor Speedway, 30, 40, 54, 64,
   76, 79, 80, 85, 101, 102, 121, 156
Indianapolis Raceway Park (IRP), 16, 142
Indianapolis Speedrome, 11
Indy 200, 30, 39, 64
International Karting Federation (IKF), 10
IRL championship, 40, 44, 49, 73, 102,
   124, 156
IRP Silver Crown race, 17
Irwin, Kenny, 18, 93, 96
Jarrett, Dale, 66, 106, 147
Joe Gibbs Racing, 70, 73, 75, 86, 87, 89, 108,
   111, 136, 138
Johnson, Jimmie, 107, 156
Jones, Parnelli, 36, 101, 102
Kalitta, Doug, 16, 17
Kenseth, Matt, 67, 74, 143, 145, 146, 156
Kenyon, Mel, 21
Knoxville Nationals, 54, 109
Labonte, Bobby, 62–64, 66, 68, 71–76, 81, 82,
   89, 91, 108, 134, 145, 147
Labonte, Terry, 152
Las Vegas 500, 42
Las Vegas Motor Speedway, 40, 46
Lazier, Buddy, 31–33, 36, 37, 51
Leary Boys, 15
Leffler, Jason, 97
Leslie, Ben, 141
Lewis, Steve, 17, 97
Lorenzen, Fred, 58
Lowe's Motor Speedway, 114, 149
Luyendyk, Arie, 34, 35, 37, 51
Makar, Jimmy, 62, 63, 64, 71, 72, 75
Marlin, Sterling, 117, 141
Martin, Mark, 74, 76, 116, 133, 141, 143
Martz, Larry, 24, 88
McCluskey, Roger, 21
McMurray, Jamie, 107
Mears, Rick, 103
Menard, John, 31, 39, 45, 46, 61, 64,
   67, 73, 104
Michigan 500, 30, 35

Michner, Andy, 12, 19, 21
NASCAR Winston Cup championship, 124, 138
Newman, Ryan, 97, 156
Niebel, Glen, 16–18, 88
Parsons, Benny, 58
Parsons, Johnny, 15, 21
Pavement Nationals, 24
Pearson, David, 58
Pepsi Coliseum, 116
Petty, Richard, 116, 120, 122, 143, 152
Phoenix International, 80, 92, 97, 100, 141
Pocono International Raceway, 149, 151
Pond, Lenny, 58
Pontiac, 52, 53, 67, 74, 75, 81, 86, 88, 89, 151
Potter team, 15, 17
Primestar 500, 67
Ranier, Harry, 58, 62, 63, 73, 85
Ranier/Walsh Racing, 52–54
Raybestos Rookie of the Year, 85, 87
Reiser, Robbie, 145, 146
Richmond International Raceway, 77, 85, 87,
   109, 128, 144, 150
Richmond, Tim, 52
Roberts, Fireball, 58
Rockingham Race Track, 74, 84, 122
Roush Racing, 74
Roush, Jack, 134, 141, 146
Rudd, Ricky, 133, 141
Rushville, Indiana, 54, 79
Rutherford, Johnny, 32, 36, 51
Ruttman, Troy, 36, 37
Salazar, Eliseo, 32, 49, 51
Sharp, Scott, 32, 36, 37, 38, 51
Silver Crown championships, 40, 54, 64
Snider, George, 18, 42, 97, 98
Stewart, Nelson, 79, 85
Talladega Superspeedway, 76, 87
Team Menard, 38, 43, 49, 50, 54, 56, 61–63,
   66, 79, 85, 102, 104
Terre Haute Action Track, 11, 12, 21, 42
Texas Motor Speedway, 67, 144
TranSouth Financial Services 400, 67
Tri-City Speedway, 16
True Speed Enterprises, 90
Turkey Night Grand Prix, 21
United Midget Racing Association (UMRA), 15
Unser, Al Jr., 57, 60
Unser, Al Sr., 32, 61
USAC Midget Rookie of the Year, 11
USAC Midget Championship, 12
USAC National Midget Championship, 15
USAC Sprint Rookie of the Year, 16
USAC Triple Crown, 52, 79
Vukovich, Bill, 101, 102, 104, 105
Wallace, Rusty, 70, 90
Waltrip, Darrell, 58, 107, 120, 127
Ward, Jeff, 47, 49
World Karting Association (WKA), 10, 15
Yarborough, Cale, 58, 85
Yates, Robert, 66
Zipadelli, Greg, 64, 71, 74, 81, 86–89, 117,
   141, 143–147

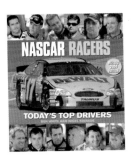
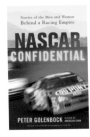
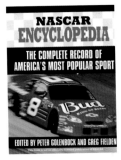

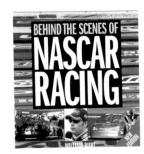
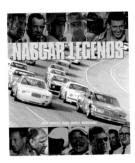

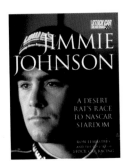